MISSISSIPPI
JUKE JOINT
Confidential

MISSISSIPPI JUKE JOINT
Confidential

House Parties, Hustlers & the Blues Life

ROGER STOLLE | *Photographs by Lou Bopp*

THE
History
PRESS

Published by The History Press
Charleston, SC
www.historypress.com

Copyright © 2019 by Roger Stolle
All rights reserved

First published 2019

Manufactured in the United States

ISBN 9781467141574

Library of Congress Control Number: 2019935351

Notice: The information in this book is true and complete to the best of our knowledge. It is offered without guarantee on the part of the author or The History Press. The author and The History Press disclaim all liability in connection with the use of this book.

All rights reserved. No part of this book may be reproduced or transmitted in any form whatsoever without prior written permission from the publisher except in the case of brief quotations embodied in critical articles and reviews.

CONTENTS

Foreword, by Jeff Konkel   7
Preface   9
Acknowledgements   15

Isn't Every Blues Club a "Juke Joint"?   17
Welcome to Wonder Light City   30
If the Walls Could Talk, Part I   41
Moonshine aka White Whiskey   62
The Death of Po Monkey's   71
The Juke Joint Hotel?   81
Red's Lounge…and Attitude   94
If the Walls Could Talk, Part II   105
100 Men DBA Hall   126
Taking Juke Joints on Tour   134
Juke Joint Festival   154

Bibliography   163
Index   169
About the Author and the Photographer   173

FOREWORD

There's no substitute for the real thing.

The first juke joint I ever stepped foot in was Green's Lounge on the south side of Memphis, located just across from a sprawling junkyard. From the outside, the place wasn't much to look at. A quick glance inside offered little to improve my opinion: dim lights, concrete floors, a low-slung ceiling and an odds-and-ends assortment of wobbly tables and mismatched chairs. But the cover charge was cheap and the beers were ice cold and came by the quart, so we settled into a darkened corner and waited for the house band, the legendary Fieldstones, to kick off their weekly gig.

I won't bore you with details about that night's performance. I couldn't even if I wanted to. Many of my memories of that night are lost to the fog of time and Budweiser. What I can tell you is that I left Green's that night—or maybe early the next morning—a changed man. I'd seen plenty of blues performances before, but never in a place like that—a place so charged with electricity and sweat and sex and booze. In other words, a juke joint.

That night was a triggering event in my two-decade journey into the heart of the real blues. A few years later, I founded Broke & Hungry Records as a vehicle for recording the kind of hard, pure blues I heard that night at Green's.

At around the same time, I met Roger Stolle, whose blues credentials are too long and varied to do them justice here. When we crossed paths in 2005, he had already started his world-famous blues store Cat Head Delta Blues & Folk Art and had cofounded the world's best blues event, Juke Joint Festival—both in Clarksdale, Mississippi. I little realized then that he was just getting started.

Foreword

Before too long, Roger and I were bumming around together at juke joints and house parties throughout the Mississippi Delta and Hill Country regions. We spent time with as many of the old blues players as we could, and we were always on the hunt for obscure talent and off-the-beaten-path clubs. No lead was too small. No trail was too cold. We eventually collaborated on two feature-length documentary films—*M for Mississippi* and *We Juke Up in Here!*—as well as a ten-part web series called *Moonshine & Mojo Hands*. All three projects celebrate the thrilling world of blues music, blues culture and blues venues.

Those are just the tip of the iceberg of the great blues-related projects Roger has been a part of. Whether he's hosting a radio show or penning a music column, producing a record or organizing a tour, he's constantly proving his knowledge and understanding of this uniquely American art form.

There is no better guide to this world than Roger. So pour yourself a glass of something strong and settle down for a great read.

–Jeff Konkel of Broke & Hungry Records

PREFACE

Welcome to my second book for The History Press. If you don't already have my previous volume, *Hidden History of Mississippi Blues*, I encourage you to pick it up. Both of these books are standalone texts, but when combined, they strive to cover a lot of deep blues territory, often from a firsthand perspective.

My first book mostly comprised general history chapters and musician interviews, along with some stunning photos by Lou Bopp. This time around, as the title implies, *Mississippi Juke Joint Confidential* seeks to delve below the murky surface of juke joint culture to tell the tales, canonize the characters and explain the special brand of blues found inside these quasi-legal establishments. A mix of history, anecdote and discovery, I won't be able to tell you where *all* the bodies are buried, but I'll certainly do my best to both educate and entertain.

The Search for Authenticity in Blues

As I stated in *Hidden History of Mississippi Blues*:

> *"Juke joint." Two words often used, often abused. They contain an inherent promise of something real, something edgy, something from another time. Many music venues of suspect authenticity coin this*

phrase at one time or another—sometimes on a sign out front, other times in advertising.

Just as blues music itself is part and parcel of the culture that spawned it, the juke joint is as much a part of history's authentic blues landscape and people as is the state of Mississippi.

Note my use of *authenticity* and *authentic* in the above excerpt. I firmly believe that this search for what's real, what's honest, what's authentic, is central to today's increasing interest in deep blues culture. More and more, visitors come to the Mississippi Delta from around the globe in search of a genuine juke joint experience.

Consumer expert and author Joseph Pine actually has a phrase for this modern consumer quest. He calls it the "experience economy," which is an economy based around perceived authenticity. On NPR's *Ted Talk Radio Hour* with Guy Raz in 2014, Pine gave the example of hotel, airline and hospital advertising. "If you could check into the ads, you'd have a great experience," he said. Unfortunately, you cannot.

Similarly, many make claims of "juke joints" and "authentic blues" only to offer up burger shacks and music closer to rock than roots. Some customers and music fans are fooled, but many are not. They may not know exactly what they're looking for, yet, but they know that ain't it.

To further quote Pine, "Increasingly, what will make us happy is spending our time and our money satisfying the desire for authenticity."

CHECK YOUR INHIBITIONS AT THE DOOR

That desire for authenticity in blues is what brought me to the door of Climmie's Western Inn in a tough part of North St. Louis in 1995. The homemade flyer said, "Where Mississippi blues people come to party," or something to that effect, implying that this was *the* music spot for African Americans who'd migrated from the Magnolia State and missed the music of "home."

The building was old but well loved. An exterior wall featured a musical mural with the "Climmie's Western Inn" name painted in large letters. Of course, the business was not an inn and was not western themed. But it was run by a take-no-prisoners, suffer-no-fools lady called Miss Climmie. The business was a juke joint.

Preface

Inside was an all-black crowd of locals, mostly from the neighborhood, mostly middle-aged and up. The band that night was Big George & the Houserockers. (For more on that night and Big George Brock, please see the final section of my *Hidden History* book.)

I won't pretend that everyone welcomed me and my then wife, but most did. For some, I suppose we looked like a couple of thrill-seeking yuppies crashing someone else's party. Maybe there's some truth in that, but I prefer to think about it like I do international travel. Why do we fly to Europe or Asia or other exotic destinations? We do it as part of our life's journey. We do it to meet new people and explore strange lands. We do it to immerse ourselves in other cultures in the hope that we emerge a little wiser and a little better for it. We do it in a search for authenticity.

"Big" George Brock plays with veteran blues drummer Frank Vick during *We Juke Up in Here!* filming at Red's. *Lou Bopp.*

Preface

Juke Joint Confidential...Literally

Generally speaking, juke owners, musicians and customers are what my late father used to call "real characters." And I love characters. Characters, to me, are authentic people who are living life, not just living. They are folks who often exist on the fringes of the modern world, just doing what they do. They are who they are, and perhaps as a result, they always have amazing stories to tell. Hopefully, I do my juke joint friends—real characters, every one of them—justice.

To that end, in some cases, these stories of the hustlers (and the hustled) in the juke joint realm can only be hinted at, so in that spirit...

I won't talk about the morning I permanently loaned an elderly bluesman forty dollars after a "lady of the evening" rolled him for his juke joint gig money. "I can't go home with no money," he explained with no sense of irony.

I won't talk about another morning when I bailed a blues friend out of jail after his car inexplicably demolished some city signs on the drive home from his otherwise lovely evening at a local juke. "I'd only had a few," he said.

I won't talk about another blues buddy who got picked up attempting to drive home from his favorite juke, got a friend to post bail and then asked the driver to drop him right back at the juke joint that led to the issue in the first place.

I won't talk about the early-morning hours after a house party gig when a harmonica player driving his "day job" newspaper route raced over a hill only to meet the side of an unfortunate horse taking an illicit moonlit ride.

I won't talk about the evening I took a down-on-his-luck bluesman to a local dollar store to buy "necessities" that turned out to be underwear and religious candles. (The young lady at checkout just kept staring at me.)

I won't talk about the night that a large female dancer suddenly ripped off her tight-knit dress to shake it for the band (who visibly winced) before the juke owner got control of the situation—and its many moving parts.

I won't talk about the night a bluesman encouraged his dancing daughters to ride each other like horses to punctuate his song, only to be faced with a major wardrobe malfunction—which didn't even pause the action.

Preface

No. I won't be telling these stories. I only hint at them here to stress the unpredictable, unforgettable, almost unimaginable nature of the juke joint life—a life lived by true blues characters, 24/7.

Welcome to what Alan Lomax called the "Land Where Blues Began." Welcome to my world, y'all.

ACKNOWLEDGEMENTS

Special thanks to my wonderful parents and extended family for their love and support.

Thanks to The History Press for once again asking me to write a book about blues music and culture I love.

Additional appreciation goes to all my blues friends and associates—especially Jeff Konkel (and his amazing family) and Lou Bopp. Also, thanks to Frank McKenna for holding down the Cat Head fort while I worked on this project and to all my partners in crime who help put on our annual Juke Joint Festival, most notably Nan Hughes (and family), Bubba O'Keefe and Goldie Hirsberg.

Kudos to all the blues players and juke joint runners who provided the anecdotes contained in these pages. As you read their names, know that they are my heroes and heroines. They have helped keep the blues alive far beyond an often-assumed expiration date. One especially loud shout-out goes to my favorite blues grouch, Mr. Red Paden. Red, you'll never know how much your decaying old party place has meant to me through the years. "The game's for life!"

Finally, thanks to my beloved blues pugs, Sadie and Ayler, for never judging my musical tastes and only occasionally soiling the rug.

From Lou Bopp
Thanks to Roger Stolle, Jeff Konkel and The History Press; all the musicians who appeared in front of my camera and put music in our ears; and my family, including the sweetest of them all, Joanna and Rose.

ISN'T EVERY BLUES CLUB A "JUKE JOINT"?

When visiting music fans drop by my Cat Head blues store on their arrival in Clarksdale, Mississippi, they are as likely to be looking for "live" music information as they are pre-recorded albums, history books or blues art. Often, they'll ask about any juke joints that might be running that night—even if they aren't entirely sure what makes a juke a juke.

After all, every juke joint is a blues club, but not every blues club is a juke joint. If you're chomping down on a bacon cheeseburger at a House of Blues as you read this chapter, please know that you are most definitely not sitting in a juke joint.

What Is a "Juke Joint," Anyway?

The true juke joint, like true blues music, comes from the African American culture of the Old South, most famously Mississippi. That is not to say that whites haven't run the occasional juke catering to black clientele or that juke joints haven't existed in more urban, big city environments. I have witnessed and enjoyed both. Still, at the end of the day, even in the modern melting pot we call America, there are a handful of cultures that have survived in virtual vacuums.

I usually tell folks that a juke (sometimes spelled "jook") joint is basically a house party where the juke host doesn't trust you to come to his (or

Many classic juke joints feature hand-painted signs telling customers what to do or, more commonly, what not to do. *Lou Bopp.*

her) actual house, so he has a little "home away from home" building that is either out in the countryside or "on the other side of the tracks." In the old days, such juke joints would have been awash with moonshine and gambling on the weekends. Low lights, cigarette smoke and a lack of cameras would have obscured the goings-on, keeping the blues parties just like Vegas. What happened there, stayed there. (As an aside, older locals here in my adopted home still occasionally refer to our town as "ClarksVegas.")

Unfortunately, today there are very few authentic, long-running juke joints left in the South that feature "live" blues music on a regular basis. But there are some. Of course, while most of the venue details are nearly as they always were, at least one thing has changed for the better.

As self-proclaimed "King of the Juke Joint Runners," Clarksdale's Red Paden, often says, "There used to be lots of cuttin' and shootin'. Now? It's like going to church." In other words, the surviving longtime jukes are safe and perhaps even a bit spiritual these days.

Following are a few things to think about on your quest for a genuine juke joint experience:

- Juke joints do not typically have phone numbers or regular hours. They rarely have "Open" signs. They don't always have up-to-date business licenses from local government. They are almost assuredly not "up to code" or insured and probably weren't built by anyone who's ever uttered the word *architect*. They may or may not have a permit to sell beer, but they will sell beer. They almost definitely won't have a liquor license, although you may well be offered the hard stuff (moonshine, perhaps?) by the owner or another guest, usually at no charge.

- Jukes and their blues house party brethren exist on the margins of the modern world. These are cash economies. Please don't pull out your platinum credit card and expect to get served anything more that an expletive from the bartender.

- Some jukes offer barbecue or soul food sales, although you shouldn't waste time looking for a health department permit on the wall. Still, while juke joints have a historically lawless reputation (deservedly), the proprietor usually does have an actual set of rules for customer behavior. Sometimes the rules are painted colorfully on the juke's walls almost as decoration (for example, "no table hopping, no mooching"), but most of the time you don't really know the rules until you break them.

- Juke joints almost never have "Juke Joint" in their names. If there is any word indicating a building or business, it is more likely to be "Inn" or "Lounge" or "Spot" or "Place." Many if not most jukes have the current or a one-time owner's name in the title—like Red's, Wild Bill's or Gip's.

After all, it ain't the planks but the people that make a juke a juke.

Juke Joint People: Anything but Average

These are not your average people. These are juke joint people—entrepreneurs with an edge, hustlers with a taste for blues. They are a special kind of tough yet good-humored folks who mostly navigate around

The relaxed nature of real-deal juke joints means that sometimes even audience members jump up to sing a song. *Lou Bopp.*

A juke joint regular shows her love for her favorite party place in Clarksdale as owner Red Paden laughs it off. *Lou Bopp.*

trouble, but when it hits head-on, they have the means to muscle through the mayhem.

Historically, these juke runners were often enterprising music fans who grew up when blues was king. Many heard work songs in the cotton fields during the week, spirituals at church on Sunday and blues in juke joints on Saturday night.

The modern juke joint owes its existence to a challenging period in southern agricultural history: the sharecropping era.

A Note on Mississippi Sharecropping

Sharecropping in the Mississippi Delta developed after the Civil War as a way for white landowners, or planters, to satisfy the cotton industry's enormous post-slavery needs. The planters allowed sharecroppers to work the land in exchange for a place to live, yearly furnish and share of the profits. In theory, if you worked hard, Mother Nature cooperated and the harvest was good, then you would be rewarded. In practice, the risky nature of farming and the dishonesty of many planters led to a system whereby workers often lived in primitive shacks and never quite made enough money at harvest time to escape what was essentially a form of bondage.

As *American Experience* described it in "Sharecropping in Mississippi," "At the end of the year, sharecroppers settled accounts by paying what they owed from any earnings made in the field. Since the plantation owners kept track of the calculations, rarely would sharecroppers see a profit." Meanwhile, many planters became quite wealthy.

According to *Living Blues* magazine founder Jim O'Neal in his article "Clarksdale Moan," "Clarksdale newspaper articles from the 1920s refer to Clarksdale as the Magic City, Wonder City of the Delta....Clarksdale made boasts, exaggerated though they may have been, of having the most millionaires per capita of any city." (An older Clarksdale customer once told me of a nearby planter who used to pull visitors into his office, where this "self-made man" would show them bank documents proving he was a millionaire.)

The most successful of these plantations developed much like small cities and included their own churches and juke joints. In some cases, larger plantations even had their own post offices, direct access to railroad lines and even money—called scrip—that could only be spent on the plantation.

By the 1940s, the growing mechanization of the cotton industry and the increasing migration of African Americans northward found the Mississippi Delta at a bit of a crossroads. As the article "Mississippi Delta Planters and Debates Over Mechanization, Labor, and Civil Rights in the 1940s" in *The Journal of Southern History* described it, "Delta planters in the 1940s wrestled with how best to modernize the plantation economy while preserving a society based on a definition of citizenship that excluded a majority of the population."

Tough times, tough subject. In fact, it is a complex conversation too big for this book. (For more on the subject, see the "Cotton Lives" chapter in *Hidden History of Mississippi Blues*.) But it is one that undeniably underpins the music we call blues.

I'm still amazed by the number of blues musicians and juke owners I've interviewed since moving to the Delta who could provide me with firsthand accounts of cotton farming, sharecropping inequities and shotgun shack life. It is a living, breathing history that continues to

Jukes commonly inhabit recycled buildings, including this old Clarksdale gas station (complete with non-functioning pumps). *Lou Bopp.*

inform the society, economy and music here. Time may heal old wounds, but it takes exactly that—time.

Understanding such history does help to explain the rise of the juke joint, the house party and the blues. Hard physical labor requires a balance. It requires an outlet, a pressure valve. Today, we have bumper stickers and memes that say, "Work hard, play hard." Back in the day, we had juke joints.

While the civil rights movement of the 1960s may have fueled huge leaps in equality here, it could not shield the Delta from the inevitable changes in technology and business that would affect everything from where folks live to what they do for entertainment.

The Times They Are a-Changin'

In his essential Mississippi guidebook, *Blues Traveling*, author Steve Cheseborough described modern juke joint business challenges this way: "The mechanized cotton harvester took away the sharecroppers' work, sending most of them up North for factory jobs. And more recently, the casinos took away what was left of the Saturday night good-time crowd. And meanwhile the end of rigid segregation gave black people alternatives to hanging out in jook joints."

I would also add that the generational evolution of black music in the South (as elsewhere) has moved the culture away from traditional blues and toward the modern genres of R&B, soul and hip-hop—often with an emphasis on deejays versus "live" bands in club settings.

This perfect storm has left little room for the juke joint in modern African American society. And for the juke joint and traditional blues to really and truly stay "alive," it must remain somehow attached to its founding culture. After all, the real will always stand out against the facsimile.

Authenticity in Traditional Jukes

"Juke joint." Think of it a bit like "Champagne" or "Parmigiano-Reggiano." To be deemed authentic, the bubbly beverage or chunky cheese must come from a particular place, a particular environment. One might even say it must come from a particular people.

Juke joint owners are not average people. They are music fans, humorists, hustlers and self-taught entrepreneurs. *Lou Bopp.*

To use a very non-juke term, think of the French word *terroir*. Derived from the Latin word *terra*, meaning earth, it is most used in describing fine wine and its sense of place. As Merriam-Webster explains, it is a "combination of factors including soil, climate, and sunlight that gives wine grapes their distinctive character." Now think about blues music, think about juke joints. Sound familiar?

A central literary figure in the Harlem Renaissance, southern-born African American author Zora Neale Hurston published *Characteristics of Negro Expression* in 1934. Her essay included perhaps the first cultural descriptions of the juke joint: "Jook is the word for a Negro pleasure house. It may mean a bawdy house. It may mean the house set apart on public works where the men and women dance, drink and gamble. Often it is a combination of all these.... Musically speaking, the Jook is the most important place in America. For in its smelly, shoddy confines has been born the secular music known as blues, and on blues has been founded jazz."

English blues researcher Paul Oliver defined jukes this way in his *Blues off the Record: Thirty Years of Blues Commentary*: "Juke joints are English pubs and Western saloons without the charm of the former or the romantic appeal of the latter. They're social clubrooms to which the church members don't go…unappealing, decrepit, crumbling shacks, which never seem to have been

The author along with partners Jeff Konkel and Damien Blaylock interview juke owner Jimmy "Duck" Holmes in 2011. *Lou Bopp.*

recently, Duck has made a bigger effort to provide scheduled blues shows at various times throughout the year.

It is worth noting that Duck puts on what is probably Mississippi's oldest blues festival either on the grounds of his juke or out at his old family farm each June, and it's always a good time.

Duck also plays at Clarksdale blues festivals like April's Juke Joint Festival, August's Sunflower River Blues Festival and October's Deep Blues Festival. He also plays occasionally at Mississippi's other important, long-running juke, Red's Lounge, which we'll talk more about later.

Two other infamous jukes also get their own chapters in this book: Wonder Light City and Po Monkey's Lounge. Both are now permanently closed, but each provided a different perspective into the deep-rooted culture that leads some folks to live the juke joint blues life. But first we probably need to clear something up—a possibly confusing term in mainstream popular culture.

"Juke Joints" versus "Jukeboxes"

According to many accounts, the word *juke* was most likely derived from the Gullah word for disorderly, infamous or wicked (*joog* or *jug*), with roots in West Africa. In modern times, most people know the term from the word *jukebox*. But as Cheseborough noted in *Blues Traveling*, juke joints "are not named for the jukeboxes found in them—rather it's the other way around."

In fact, curiously enough, "jukebox" was a label that the music and manufacturing industry fought for years. Descriptions such as "coin-operated phonograph," "music vendor" or "music-playing machine" were much preferred and pushed early on. Industry leaders felt the term "jukebox" limited the relevance and respectability of their product by tying it to low-down (often small-town or rural) alcohol-fueled blues clubs.

This caused many salesmen in the business to dance around the term "jukebox" in conversations until potential new club or restaurant clients would finally say something like, "Oh, you're talking about a jukebox!" The name stuck.

Once integrated in the public's vocabulary, some in the industry laughingly tried to suggest that the term actually came from Old Europe,

Pontotoc, Mississippi's one-man blues band, Terry "Harmonica" Bean, entertains at Red's juke joint in Clarksdale, Mississippi. *Lou Bopp.*

not the Old South. The various marketing angles tried by the industry were completely unnecessary, of course, since the public loved the band-in-a-can contraptions.

With the end of national Prohibition in 1933, the jukebox industry boomed. By the end of the 1930s, it's been estimated that there may have been close to 250,000 such machines operating in the United States. (This new "cash business" did not go unnoticed by organized crime, incidentally, leading to the occasional criminal investigation.)

The spread of jukeboxes throughout the South's jukes and cafés must have been akin to the more recent spread of sports-filled flat-screen TVs in America—turning every beer joint into a "sports bar." Just as computers and robots supplement or supplant factory workers today, such new entertainment technology was seen by some as a threat to older traditions.

As author Stephen Calt described it in *I'd Rather Be the Devil*, "Musical mechanization…eroded the live blues market. Since the mid-1930s, the once-pervasive jukehouse culture of Mississippi had begun to give way to the jukebox, which all but replaced live performers." Of course, musicians still continued to play live music, often working alongside the bright, noisy boxes.

As bluesman Jimmy "Duck" Homes told me, "My mother ran [our] juke joint, and they had a jukebox. Even though people would come by and play, they still had a jukebox."

In the end, jukeboxes gained respectability and showed up in as many family settings as party settings, leading none other than President Ronald Reagan to proclaim "National Jukebox Week" in 1988. Ironically, he even referred to jukeboxes as "clean fun" in his speech, blissfully unaware of their Saturday night juke joint roots.

WELCOME TO WONDER LIGHT CITY

An old African American bluesman played Clarksdale's iconic Red's Lounge one night for what must have been his hundredth time. This particular night, the nearly eighty-year-old showman had a younger white bass player from Nashville backing him. They, along with a local drummer, sounded amazing—like Muddy Waters meets Chuck Berry meets Sam Cooke (with a touch of Albert Ayler dissonance thrown in for good measure).

At the end of the night, they packed up their gear out front of the old juke joint, and under low light and heavy mosquitos, the aging blues legend handed the bassist his pay. The sideman quickly counted the cash, decided it wasn't enough and proceeded to argue with the tall, wiry bluesman. To accent his point, the bass player raised his fists—TV boxing style, like Ali. Immediately, the old man raised his in response—boxing style circa 1930, with his arms out and knuckles up. Coming from an era where juke joint brawls were common and survival went to the fittest, reflex kicked in.

The old man threw a determined punch, striking the younger man in the head so hard that it knocked him backward, although it didn't knock him down. The punch deliverer braced himself, awaiting a knuckle-filled retort. Instead, the bass player burst out laughing. He'd just been sucker-punched by an octogenarian bluesman in a puffy wig and polyester zoot suit.

The old man dropped his fists, and the two went and sat down beside the rusting barbecue grill, leaning against the faded front wall of the ancient juke. The bluesman apologized. They talked for quite some time, agreed to play together again and headed out for the night.

The next morning, I asked the bass player, who also happened to work for me occasionally at my Cat Head store, "So, did he end up paying you more money?" He responded with a comical look of disbelief. "No. All I got was punched!" We both laughed.

And so, I introduce you to that wigged, suited (and occasionally boxing) Mississippi juke joint legend, Mr. Robert "Bilbo" Walker.

"I Just Always Wanted to Be Somebody"

People often talk about the "self-made" man or woman. Some may even claim to be such a thing. Often, they simply mean that someone took one amount of family money and made it a bigger amount—basically, generational wealth.

To me, "self-made" means just that. An individual comes from virtually nothing, without the benefits of inheritance or social standing, and through hard work and perseverance achieves goals that seemed impossible at the start. This may involve financial riches, or it may simply involve the riches of life—fame, family and feats.

One such self-made man was juke joint player turned owner Robert "Bilbo" Walker. He once told me, "I just always wanted to be somebody," and he worked every day of his life to be just that.

Eight Decades on His Way to a Juke Joint

Located seemingly in the middle of Nowhere, Mississippi, yet actually only twenty minutes from downtown Clarksdale, Bilbo's decision to build his juke joint in such a harsh landscape was a bit like the gangsters of yore deciding to build casinos in the wide-open Las Vegas desert. But since it was old family property, which he already owned, the bluesman viewed it a bit like Kevin Costner in *Field of Dreams*—if you build it, they will come. Of course, the realities of developing this swampy, wooded plot adjacent to the cotton fields where he started life would prove to be more like building Jurassic Park, as the elements continually worked against him—snakes, mosquitos, floods and outlaws. But none of that stopped him.

Few bluesmen ever wore a wig and suit like entertainer Robert "Bilbo" Walker, a man as quick with a punch as a guitar riff. *Lou Bopp.*

As the dreamer later told the producers of *Great Big Story* (www.greatbigstory.com) at his juke's grand opening in June 2017, "This is Wonder Light City. It's not really a nightclub. It's more like a juke joint. It's what the people love down in Mississippi. This is seven years I've been on this thing. It wouldn't have took that long, but it kept getting robbed, and then a flood came in and got it. I want it to be something people remember me for. I want it to become as famous as any place has ever been in the world."

Honestly, I was as amazed as anyone when Bilbo finally flipped the switch and turned on the lights. As I told *Great Big Story*, "I used to tell people there won't be any 'new' juke joints." And yet there we were, with Bilbo's joint getting grandfathered in.

So, how does a man live eighty years on earth, travel around the world, raise multiple families, work hard jobs, record blues records and in the end finally achieve his lifelong dream in such an unforgiving environment?

HOUSE PARTIES, HUSTLERS & THE BLUES LIFE

FROM COTTON FIELDS TO WORLD STAGES

"My name is Robert 'Bilbo' Walker. I was born off New Africa Road [near Clarksdale] on Kline's Plantation, February 19, 1937. Seventeen children in my family. We picked cotton, chopped cotton and stuff like that. In them days, I guess it was good. It was all we knew, anyways," he told me in an interview for *Blues Revue*. "Physically, the work was hard, I would say, because everything was done from muscles. From your backbone and your muscles, everything was done—cutting wood, sawing wood, picking the cotton and carrying the cotton to the scales. There was a lot of work in everything you did back in those days, but it was enough to keep people busy and keep people out of trouble, too."

The future blues legend and juke joint entrepreneur began his life modestly as just another anonymous field worker trying to help his family survive the Mississippi Delta's tough sharecropping system. Off and on for the rest of his life he would return to farming and actually held an affection for it—if not for the "way it was" in his days of youth.

In the mid-1950s, Bilbo decided to join the thousands of rural Mississippi plantation workers who headed north in search of non-field work and a better life. It was his Great Migration. And he would not be denied.

While he couldn't read or write, he was always street smart and quick on his feet. Initially, he landed in a small city near Chicago where he knew some of his southern relatives had migrated. He thought perhaps he could move in with them. Still, he didn't show up with his hand out. He showed up with a plan.

He found the biggest, newest building in town. He figured that such a towering structure would hold the best promise of a good job. Dressed for Sunday and with a smile on his face, he inquired about employment. The manager said that, yes, there was a job available: elevator operator.

Telling the story decades later, Bilbo laughed as he told me, "I didn't even know what an 'elevator' was, so I sure didn't know what an 'elevator operator' was!" Still, in classic "fake it 'til you make it" style, he bluffed his way into the position, practicing taking the lift up and down, stopping the elevator at just the right spots to let passengers off on the proper floors versus into a wall. After all, these were the days before "automatic" elevators.

Once his meal ticket was ensured, he left his new job in search of his relatives' address. He arrived unannounced but was warmly welcomed into the residence after promising to add another paycheck to the family's bankroll.

Later, he would work at automobile plants in the region, play gospel music on Chicago's famed Maxwell Street and jam blues in the region's many clubs. He always had a dollar and made sure folks knew it. As he once put it, "I always had me a new Cadillac, so people just knew I *must* have money. What they didn't know was that sometimes I was sleeping in that Cadillac!"

For most of his life, Bilbo held a day job and played music on the side, so it wasn't until relatively late in life that his full attention turned to blues. In the late 1990s, he started recording—first for Rooster Blues and later Fedora Records. These albums along with his legendary stage show led to festival performances both here and abroad.

In fact, I think the first I heard about Bilbo's Wonder Light City juke joint dream was on the road. As part of my Cat Head mission to "organize and promote the blues from within," I sometimes facilitate trips out of state or overseas for Mississippi bluesmen who can't easily or reliably travel on their own. They get a great payday, I get a free trip. (See my chapter on "Taking Juke Joints on Tour" for more on these fish-out-of-water adventures.)

And so, after decades of playing other people's clubs, jukes, parties and festivals, the bluesman known around the world as "Bilbo" decided that time was running out. It was time to turn a dream into reality.

The blues life is a bit of a hustle. Here juke joint legend "Bilbo" hustles a few bucks out of pool players in Alligator, Mississippi. *Lou Bopp.*

A Juke Joint Called "Wonder Light City"

When eighty-year-old Mississippi blues legend Robert "Bilbo" Walker talked about Wonder Light City in the last year of his earthly existence, his eyes lit up almost as much as his aptly named juke joint. He called the ancient blue quonset hut his lifelong dream.

Known for his flashy suits and duck-walking stage antics, the flamboyant musician envisioned a venue just as mesmerizing. Armed with nothing but his hands and his heart, he acquired a rusty old ex-army barracks somewhere in the Delta around 2009 or '10. He cut it into pieces and moved it with a cotton trailer to an old, overgrown family property on the outskirts of town.

For the better part of a decade, he worked on his dream whenever he could—painting the exterior, nailing up plywood inside and pouring concrete floors and sidewalks. He cleared forest on the property, dug fishing ponds and even built an outdoor stage suspended by trees—like a treehouse. He spread out tons of pea gravel to create a surprisingly orderly parking lot. He also hung Christmas lights—*lots* of Christmas lights—both inside and out.

At one point, a spring flood swept away much of his exterior work, including his initial attempt at a gravel parking area. The rising tide also allowed most of the catfish in his ponds to swim off into the cotton fields, never to be seen again. Still, he persevered.

He would often wake up in the middle of the night with a new idea, leave his house trailer in nearby Alligator, Mississippi, and drive out into a moonlit countryside filled with prowling wildlife and stinging insects to quietly work on his dream.

The old bluesman and entrepreneur essentially made something out of nothing. He took cast-off materials and put his back into it. Since the juke joint property lacked electricity, water and sewer, Bilbo had to innovate. He bought a couple secondhand gas-powered generators to power the thousands of Christmas lights, his musical equipment and a beer cooler.

Then he reinvented how plumbing works—or, in this case, sometimes didn't. From inside the building, the bathroom appeared normal, but a trip outside to the back of the building revealed an unusual "bucket-filling" system to give the traditional household toilet its flush. A seam in the Delta dirt showed where the improvised sewer pipe left the building, and a five-second walk led you to the wastewater's final destination: an open pit.

He actually planned to launch his old-school creation in time for Clarksdale's Juke Joint Festival in April 2016 but was met with another unexpected, nearly catastrophic setback on the road to opening.

The Tale of a Blues Highway Man

For those of y'all who don't know, Bilbo was somewhat legendary for splitting his time between Clarksdale, Mississippi, and Bakersfield, California, during the last decades of his life. Basically, he had a lengthy musical gig out in Bakersfield at one point and eventually brought his wife out. The gig went away, but he continued to maintain a residence there.

In the winter of 2016, Bilbo was in Bakersfield when I booked him a nice university gig in South Florida for that February. He was planning to come back to his native Delta in March anyway to prepare his juke for the coming festival, so driving back a month early, so we could fly out of Memphis, seemed like no big deal. But it was.

Another thing to know about Bilbo is that he loved to drive—anything, anywhere, any time. Over the two decades that I knew him, he owned everything from tractors to tour buses, limos, Corvettes, RVs and even one of those low-profile airport vehicles that tows jumbo jets.

In accordance with his gas-powered philosophy, Bilbo planned to do the 1,900-mile, twenty-six-hour drive from California to Mississippi nonstop. (He laughed at the idea of spending hard-earned money on hotel rooms.) So, he must have been a tired man by the time his pickup truck—with a car on a trailer in back—threw its timing chain in rural Oklahoma.

According to Bilbo, the truck backfired, starting a small roadside field fire, before losing power and coasting to a stop. After cursing his truck, he decided to pull his car off the trailer and head for help. Unfortunately, he blew out two tires trying to get the car off the trailer.

After a bit more cursing, he called a friend in Mississippi who managed to arrange a tow truck. As the tow truck driver stood next to Bilbo's pickup discussing options, he complimented both Bilbo's truck and the interesting signs, lights and equipment jammed into the back bed. Bilbo explained that the materials were destined for his soon-to-be juke joint in Mississippi, Wonder Light City.

Bilbo asked the driver to take him and his adopted son (who was keeping him company on the adventure) somewhere where he could buy two used tires. The tow truck took them and their car in the opposite direction of their original travel and perhaps farther than necessary, eventually pulling into a big-box discount store parking lot. Bilbo and his son got out and went inside.

At the automotive counter, they were told that the store was closing in ten minutes, but they could come back first thing in the morning. They left

Bluesman turned juke owner Robert "Bilbo" Walker celebrates his family farmland just outside Clarksdale, Mississippi. *Lou Bopp.*

the counter, thinking they might try somewhere else. Unfortunately, when they returned to the parking lot, there was no tow truck driver and no tow truck—just Bilbo's car with two flat tires.

Wintertime Comes to Oklahoma

According to Bilbo, the temperatures dropped into the thirties that night. He and his son dug an "old, dirty, thin quilt" out of the trunk and curled up together under it inside the freezing car. "My teeth were chattering like this," Bilbo told me as he reenacted the frigid evening.

As the sun rose and the retailer reopened, he went inside to do business. Since the store only sold new (not used) tires, Bilbo had to make a call back home to get some additional money wired over. After sorting out the finances, he returned to the automotive counter. Apparently, at this point, he was looking and feeling a little rough after all the stress and travel—plus, to be fair, without his puffy wig and fancy suit, our eighty-year-old blues friend could look a little menacing.

Words were said. Tempers flared. The store became reluctant to provide service. Finally, noticing "one of those things," Bilbo later told me, pointing at my store computer, "I told the man to put 'Bilbo Walker' into it. I'm famous!" Incredulously, the man typed Bilbo's name. To his surprise, multiple photos and articles came up showcasing the legendary bluesman. Suddenly, all was well.

With his steel horse re-shoed, Bilbo and his son pulled out of the parking lot. Since he grew up in a time of cotton, not education, Bilbo couldn't read any of the street signs. But as a matter of habit, he had unconsciously memorized the landmarks, turns and so on and was able to get back to where the original breakdown occurred. As he pulled up to the spot, he couldn't believe what he saw—or, rather, didn't see. His truck and trailer were gone.

In the morning sunlight, he now saw that there was a house out across a field from the road. He went over to see if anyone was home. The guy who answered the door said he saw it all. He saw Bilbo get his car towed, and a short time later, the tow truck driver returned alone to haul off the pickup. Bilbo's truck and trailer would never be seen again.

Tired and truck-less, Bilbo and his son drove silently toward Clarksdale, just looking forward to getting back to their Mississippi home. A few states later, the exhausted bluesman pulled into his Wonder Light City compound to check on things. He quickly realized that something wasn't right. His dream had been broken into. Lock and chain cut. His stuff was gone—sound equipment, freezer, stove, air compressor, generators, riding lawnmower and pretty much everything else that wasn't nailed down. Like Albert King's famous song goes, "If it wasn't for bad luck, I wouldn't have no luck at all."

To his credit, though, Bilbo was his usual unstoppable self. The next day, he told me this story with a sense of the ridiculousness of the situation—almost like he was laughing to keep from crying. He planned to deal with the tow truck service, but first he wanted to track down the local burglars.

While he failed to get his truck and trailer back, he did manage to track down a good bit of his juke joint's stolen booty. He also found out who was involved in the theft, although that was the last he reported on the subject.

It took him another year to get his Wonder Light dream back on track, but that he did. He finally told me in May 2017 that he would open in mid-June. I made him a poster and spread the word via social media.

The Culmination of a Juke Joint Life

In June 2017, the celebrated bluesman finally flipped the switch, and it was like Disneyland in a cotton field. Colorful photos and excited comments began to appear on Facebook, Instagram and Twitter. Both *Great Big Story* (Turner) and *Jazz Night in America* (NPR) featured the brand-new old-school party place. And the dreamer smiled.

The weekend of the grand opening, the eighty-year-old was tired, but he played, partied and publicized his city of lights like a man half his age. He hoped, of course, to grow his new endeavor into a popular destination—a place where he could play and make money, a place where he could throw festivals and offer camping. He dreamed big.

Around this time, he told me with a chuckle, "You know, I may never really ever be done working on this place. To tell you the truth, I enjoy it."

Sadly, while Bilbo successfully fought off Mother Nature in developing his Wonder Light City property, Father Time waits for no one. Within a month of his grand opening, Walker was diagnosed with cancer. He and his wife went out to their second home in Bakersfield to seek treatment that July

Robert "Bilbo" Walker regularly performed at Red's Lounge in Clarksdale but dreamed of playing at his own juke joint. *Lou Bopp.*

through September. In October, he returned to his beloved Delta to play his final two shows in life at Helena, Arkansas's King Biscuit Blues Festival and my own Cat Head Mini Blues Fest.

The day in between the festival dates, he also participated in a "King Biscuit Call & Response" panel discussion I moderated. He talked so enthusiastically of his blues life and his juke joint dream that everyone in attendance wanted to believe he was catching a second wind. After all his hardships in life, he still spoke in future tense. But it was not to be.

He returned again to Bakersfield to resume treatments, and in the early morning hours of November 29, 2017, the blues legend—and self-made man—passed away.

Today, on the edge of a cotton field just south of Clarksdale, Mississippi, Wonder Light City sits dark and decaying, waiting for its dreamer to return. "I always told myself I could be anything I wanted to be, could do anything I wanted to do. And so far, I proved it. All these years, I proved I could be anything I wanted to be," he told Jeff Konkel and me in our 2008 *M for Mississippi* documentary. Then, with his usual sense of humor, the bluesman who never gave up added, "Except get rich. That's the only thing I ain't never done!"

IF THE WALLS COULD TALK, PART I

Over the years, I've had the distinct pleasure of interviewing dozens of culturally connected, mostly Mississippi-born blues musicians. Such an amazing opportunity is akin to reading a history book that talks back and answers questions.

Hopefully, most of the interviewees felt the way that "Blind" Arvella Gray did when he spoke with blues researcher Paul Oliver in 1960 for Oliver's classic *Conversation with the Blues*: "I can't see you, but I'll tell you about myself because I can see you're on the level."

What follows is a loosely connected collection of interview excerpts that work together to illustrate the general nature of juke joints, house parties and the blues life. A sincere thanks goes out to each and every one of the interviewees. These folks are the real deal.

JUKE OWNER RED PADEN (CLARKSDALE, MISSISSIPPI)

I'm the bartender, the bouncer—you name it. We can have a good time in here. And that's what it's about. But you ain't fixing to mess with my money. And that's the bottom line. Out here in this juke joint, you don't have to be perfect. You can be a billionaire or you can be a poor old boy.

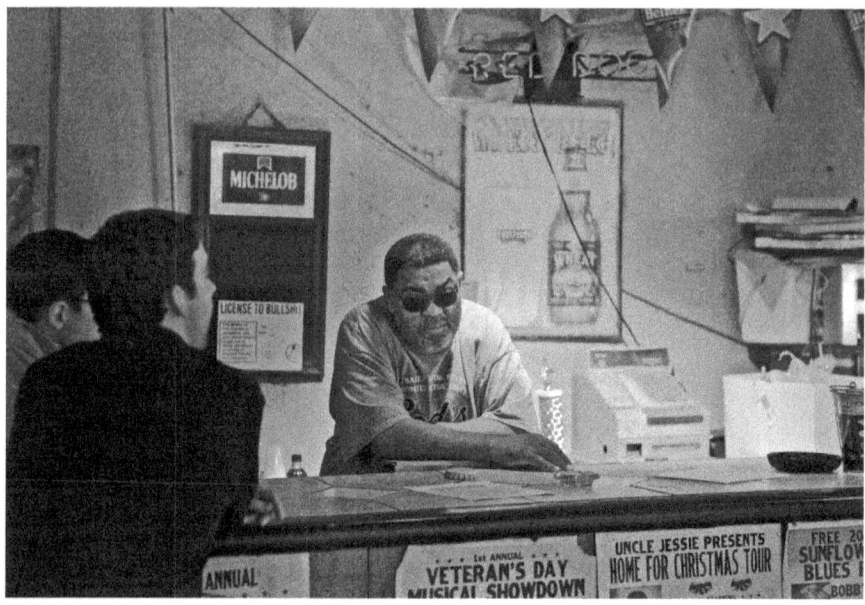

The author and Jeff Konkel take a break with juke owner Red Paden during the filming of the *We Juke Up in Here!* doc. *Lou Bopp.*

If you know how to come in here and conduct yourself like a man or woman, then you fit in here perfect. We juke up in here! We go beyond the call of duty.

"Cadillac" John Nolden (Renova, Mississippi)

Charlie Booker used to play around that time, and he used to come around Leland. He had a little place he played at down there. I forget the name of those little places. That's been a long time ago. Man, he'd have a crowd out there. He got in a fight down there one night. A woman come on with a knife. He had to fight her with the guitar. That's the only way he could keep her off him. I think he tore the strings off that guitar [laughs]. *And I think he couldn't play no more that night. He had tore up that guitar.*

John Horton (Greenville, Mississippi)

Yeah, Willie Foster was a tough guy. We used to be loading our speakers and stuff—had some long speakers—and he'd pick up two of them at the same time while two of us were wrestling with one [laughs]. *He had those big, huge hands. Back in the day, when he was drinking, boy, you talk about mean. I came up around him and T-Model Ford and them. Him and T-Model Ford, Sam Carr, sometimes Frank Frost. They'd start out railing, boy, just having a good time. We had a little juke down there in the country that we'd kind of hide at. Boy, about halfway through the night, they'd take a pistol break* [laughs]. *I've had some times with those old-timers. I was riding in a van with them once, taking them to Arcola, Mississippi, a little club. It was T-Model, Frank Frost, John Price, me and I think there was somebody else. Anyway, Frank Frost said, "I just feel like whooping me somebody tonight." T-Model pulled out a pistol and said, "Well, I hope it ain't me!"*

James "T-Model" Ford (Greenville, Mississippi)

Any fighting come up, I'm in the middle of it! I could throw some fists then. So, we went on up there. Uncle was looking at the guy that had done the whooping of him. The guy's friend came by me, came out with his knife and grabbed on to me to cut. I throwed a bottle at him. Another guy came in behind me and stabbed me in my back, and I whirled around. I got my knife out and cut his throat. His knife was burning me like a piece of hot iron. Missed my spine by that much. He died, too. I wasn't mean, but I would fight. They sent me to Trenton, Tennessee, on the chain gang. They give me ten years, but I didn't stay but two. They put me in my stall at night. During the day, if you see a snake [when clearing land on the chain gang], *you don't say nothing. If you say something, you going to catch it! Had one boy there. He had a whole lot of mouth. He seen one of them rattlesnakes laying around there. He said, "Oh, look there's a snake!" Guard said, "You found him. Now catch him!"* [Ford motions like a guard with a shotgun.] *So, it killed him* [Ford acts out being bitten by a snake].

Terry "Harmonica" Bean (Pontotoc, Mississippi)

I played with T-Model Ford about three years before I broke off on my own. One night in Moorehead [outside a juke] *we got robbed. I had told him about taking the money and just walking out with it. The guy ran right by me as I was loading my stuff up, and T-Model said I was in with him 'cause I didn't grab the guy when he come by!* [Laughs.] *Then, we went on down to Greenville on Nelson Street, and he got beat up a couple times down there. You know, I'd try to get people off of him. Aw man, I said if I don't get out of this stuff, I'm going to be mixed up amongst them, so I had to ease on out. So that's how we left it. When I left him, me and Asie Payton played for a year. Me and T-Model was in Indianola one night playing, and Asie Payton came in about half drunk. Well, he wasn't drunk, but he was about lit. He wanted to play T-Model's guitar, but T-Model wouldn't let him because he owed him money from about thirty years ago and ain't paid it. T-Model wanted that money back. It was a big mess. So, I told him, "Let him play. I want to hear him." And that's how me and Asie kicked it off.*

Cedell Davis (Arkansas/Mississippi)

Fights would break out back then. I knowed the guy well that got shot, and I knowed the guy that shot him. The guy got stabbed on top of that. A guy called Geechie. He got shot and stabbed, and they thought he was dead. I thought about it, and I said, "Well, feel his pulse." A lot of them didn't even know what a pulse was, man [laughs]. *I told them, "In his arm." They felt his arm and said, "No, he ain't dead." Next thing you know, the guy sat up. The fight was about another guy called Hop-Along butting into his business. On a Saturday, all of the people from the surrounding areas would be in Helena. If you had the money everything was there for you. Gambling. Numbers rackets. Ladies. If you had the money, they could accommodate you. And there was music at just about every place. People played on the streets, too.*

BILL ABEL (DUNCAN, MISSISSIPPI)

Fights and scary instances? There was a bunch of them. One of them was when we went to play at a place called the White Eagle in Yazoo City. Tommy Hollins and W.H. was riding with me. It was me and the drummer, Wade Loper. We was the only two white guys. And it was at Paul "Wine" Jones's sister's juke joint in Yazoo City. Paul lined it up. We get down there, and Tommy goes, "I didn't know we was coming here. I ain't going in there to play." So, I'm thinking, "If you're not going in there, I'm sure not going in there!" The place had been roped off with police tape, and there was these guys that was walking around the edge like guard dogs. She had sold tickets and said, "No riff raff. We're having blues tonight." 'Cause it was an all-out juke joint with a lot of drugs outside and people getting killed and stuff, you know. So, she had roped it all off to protect us, she said. We went on in, and this big old guy kept following me around all night. Every time I'd go to the bathroom, he'd follow me into the bathroom, so I was worried. "What's he doing following me into the bathroom?" Then, I figured it out. He was my bodyguard. I said, "You're my bodyguard, aren't you?" He said, "Yeah, you got nothing to worry about. Ain't nobody going to lay a finger on you. They got to go through me." So, we all had our own personal bodyguards.

JOHN HORTON

The number one place for [juke joint violence] *was Glen Allan, Mississippi. God. They still got a bad reputation. They're a little better now. We had went in there and set up and played one song and had to go out the back door and leave our stuff* [laughs]. *Glen Allan has done had that reputation. You talk to anybody down my way—even my father back in his day. I don't know what it is about that little area. When we first started riding around in that little town, we wouldn't even get out. It was rowdy like. One of the nights, we had just played and took a break. We were just sitting at a table talking, and all of the sudden a shot went off, and we thought it was just like a firecracker. We didn't hear no argument or something to lead up to that, so we just sat there, and, "Pow!" We looked*

"Big" George Brock has played in—and even owned—juke joints on and off for much of his nearly ninety years. *Lou Bopp.*

around by the pool table, and one of the guys was getting up, trying to get a pool stick to go at the guy with the pistol [laughs]. *And his partner was standing over there saying, "Fool, you're shot. Let me take you over to the hospital." It was like that song "Tin Pan Alley": "Tin Pan Alley is the baddest place in town. They start cutting and shooting as soon as the sun goes down"* [laughs].

"BIG" GEORGE BROCK (MISSISSIPPI/MISSOURI)

When I opened up my joint, I just did that for a living. It was just a vacant building, and I went and asked the landlord, "Could I rent that place?" He said, "Yeah, but you got to fix it up." It took me a year to get it in shape. Police Johnson used to own it. It was the Earlybird Lounge for quite a while. They wouldn't give me a license for but six months since so much had been happening there. It was a bad neighborhood. They used to call it the Bucket of Blood 'cause somebody would get hurt there every weekend. They told me, "If you don't have a lot of problems in six months, we'll give you a license for a year." So after that, I got a license for a year and went on.

SAM CARR (LULA, MISSISSIPPI)

One day, he wanted me to work the door at a show, so he paid me for working the door. I was larger than I am now. Great big muscles. Playing out at this old man's place [in Helena], *he was running colored and white, anybody who wants to come in, which that* [integration] *really wasn't happening, but he did it. I was bad back then. A big shot. So I come over here in Mississippi, and I stole my papa Garfield Carr's army .45. Everywhere I go, I have to show that gun. Some ol' bad boys might try to run me off the door. I kept that pistol right here* [points to his waistband]. *"I take that," they'd say. "You might take what's in it!" "Ain't nothing in it, no how." Pow! Tin rattle on top the house. "Put that away, boy, or you gonna kill somebody!" Said, "That's what I intend to do if you try to take it." Had no more trouble out of nobody, taking that fifty cents at the door.*

ROBERT KIMBROUGH SR. (HOLLY SPRINGS, MISSISSIPPI)

At our place, there weren't a lot of fights. It was more like home. Everybody got along in there. I'm not saying a fight never broke out. You know, somebody going to always get out of pocket, but we check that. We'd dance. We'd eat and drink, and when it was over with, everybody'd go home. The juke joint burned down in 2000. We don't know to this day what happened. We had gotten the place [after his father, Junior Kimbrough, died in 1998] *and opened it up on Friday, Saturday and Sunday nights. Friday night was David's night, Saturday night was my night and Sunday night was Kinney's night. So, that Sunday, we had a really big night. After we left, Kinney called me about six or seven in the morning. He said, "Robert, you need to get down to the club!" He was very upset and just hung the phone up. I jumped in the car, and I was flying down this road trying to see what's going on. I got there, and man, it was just...gone. Everything. Burned to the ground.*

R.L. BOYCE (COMO, MISSISSIPPI)

Junior Kimbrough's juke joint, oh, man. I just about stayed there. Paid rent there. Water bill, gas bill, all that! [Laughs.] *You'd go out there to Junior's place back then. The door was open for everybody. Didn't make no difference who you was or where you come from. If Rural* [R.L. Burnside] *didn't play, I played. If I didn't play, Junior played. Anybody. It just keep right on jumping. You knew you had to go to work on Monday morning, but you'd be right there. Headache hanging over. Like I said, good time! Good time. Now, Jessie Mae Hemphill was the first lady I played with. I used to be her drummer back then. She-Wolf? I played with her on that album. "Standing in My Back Door Crying." Yeah, Jessie Mae and me did that song together. Whew man, that was a mean woman! You got to come right with her. If it ain't right, she don't want it.*

Steve "Lightnin'" Malcolm (North Mississippi)

The first day I met R.L. Burnside was, like, monumental. I just remember everybody being quiet when Jack Owens and them was playing, but this one guy kept talking. "Don't be so evil. Don't be so mean!" And we kept thinking, "Man, I wish that guy would be quiet." You know how it is. This guy is loud over there, and his voice stands out. Next thing you know, he's got the guitar. I just remember thinking that the only way he's leaving here is in the back of a police car [laughs]. That was just the image I had of him in my mind. It was just like, "This dude is crazy." It was like a train just rolling over you.

Martin "Big Boy" Grant (Senatobia, Mississippi)

My mother was from Mississippi, so after my daddy died, we moved back to Wyatt, Mississippi—deep in the Hill Country, right next to Chulahoma where Junior Kimbrough's juke was. But I didn't really go to his club 'til I got up and grown—well, high school age, anyway. Then, I started going out to it. It was fun to get to see Junior and R.L. playing, but Sunday night was the only night they did it. You could drive by at seven or eight o'clock, and it looked like an abandoned building. You go by at ten or eleven, and they were parked for a mile, lined up on the side of the highway. And it was just full-out hot in the summertime and cold in the wintertime. They did have a fire in the winter, but all they had was a fan to suck the heat out in the summer. They'd stay out there 'til two, three or four o'clock in the morning playing out there. This was the last club Junior had. When he died, Kinney and David Kimbrough took it over, and then it burned down.

Steve "Lightnin'" Malcolm

After I met R.L., he said, "Come out to Junior Kimbrough's juke [in Chulahoma, Mississippi]," and we'd go out there and play. I was kind of traveling all over, you know, booking my little jobs. I was traveling around Arkansas a lot, going to Texas every once and a while. Go up through Missouri, Kansas City. Places like that. I'd get down here maybe a couple times a year. I wish I would have hung out there more. When I got the call, Sherman Cooper [a promoter in Como] *called me about three in the morning. He said, "Damn it, Junior Kimbrough's joint just burned down." I just hung up the phone and looked at the wall. It was almost like getting the news that your brother had just died. It really hurt. Man, that place was awesome. Anything was liable to be happening. Women be dancing. It seemed like every note that was played up in there was at maximum intensity. There was no messing around. You had to go all the way for broke. That carries over to when we go out and play places now. We try to remember it. I never got to hang with Junior too much. I just really know Junior through his music, which is a big influence on the music I make.*

Martin "Big Boy" Grant

They said Junior's building used to be an old church, so you had these little side areas where they had couches and stuff set up. It had little posts and beams—kind of like a little shed coming off a house—and then the stage was on the other side of the room from those little dugouts, in its own little dugout. It had its own swinging doors at one time at the front of it, but then they took those down because it was too much trouble getting all your stuff in and out. It was pretty cool. The drums were in an alcove off to the side, like a hall going to side door where all the musicians hung out off to the side. Or, most the time during the summer, they went outside 'cause it was a lot cooler outside. But it was a fun place. It had paintings all up on the wall. They had one of like Oprah. You know, they had some soul pictures—"good times" pictures—and then Miller Lite signs and all kind of beer signs. There was a pool table right there as you walk in. Then the bar was in the back.

SEAN "BAD" APPLE (SARAH, MISSISSIPPI)

I finally moved to Mississippi for good in October 2006. That's when I met R.L. Boyce of Como. I played with him and Martin "Big Boy" Grant and others throughout the North Mississippi Hill Country. We played like Marshandra's juke [that was in a mobile home] *out in Marshall County. It was small, but they'd get like eighty-five people in there—dancing and drinking and gambling. It burned down to the ground. Another real favorite place of mine was blues singer Mary Ann "Action" Jackson's brother Rooster's place. He was in his seventies and had thirty-six children. It was a makeshift juke joint near Sardis with picnic tables, a wood-burning stove and a disco ball or two. My other favorite juke is Red's Lounge in Clarksdale. Every time I play there, I tell the audience to give Red a big round of applause. Because whether blues is popular or unpopular at a given time, it doesn't matter to a guy like Red. He says, "This game's for life," and as long as he's here, his doors are open for blues music to be played. It's that kind of hush-hush, this side of the tracks thing that is actually bringing a lot of European tourists. It's almost like, "I don't know. Is it safe to go in this place?" And then you get inside and find three-hundred-pound women doing crazy, dirty dancing* [laughs].

MARY ANN "ACTION" JACKSON (SENATOBIA, MISSISSIPPI)

Now, my brother "Rooster" owns a juke joint in Sardis, Mississippi. That's a good one! You know those [pre-fabricated] *garages you can get? The ones you pull your car under? He and his son took one of those garages and put concrete up under it. They just put a concrete slab, and then they boxed it in and attached it to a trailer house. So, one part is the trailer house, and one part is the garage. He put the garage and then the trailer house up behind that* [forming a "T"]. *And it keeps getting better and better. We have to get back down through there with the band. My brother had been doing blues parties all the time, but they used to be at his house—like house parties.*

Drummer Frank Vick, harmonica legend "Big" George Brock and a friend rest up before a big blues show at Red's. *Lou Bopp.*

Martin "Big Boy" Grant

Then there's Mary Ann "Action" Jackson's brother's place. It's a single-wide trailer with the side cut out of it in the middle. Then there's like a three- or four-car portable garage married up to the side of it and filled in with boards on the outside to make it a room. Down there in the room are all the picnic tables, dance floor and everything. The trailer itself is the stage 'cause it's setting up about three or four feet off the ground, and steps come up to it. It wouldn't be so bad if you didn't have to come up to it to go to the bathroom or to the kitchen or to the table they're playing craps or cards on the other side. You know? So, everybody walks up and cuts right through the middle of the band! But it's a real cool place. In the wintertime, he has two big barrels, big stoves, to heat the place—and it'll glow cherry red, where you have to open up all the doors in order to cool it down enough to stay in there. It's kickin' hot up in there.

Red Paden

Red's, it's just for a family outing. That's the reason I have the building down there. I'm not making any money, but it's a place for me to get away from home. It's a comfortable place to come and sit in. A lot of times you hear negative input. That's what a lot of people want you to believe is going on. You notice that it's a nice place with older guys letting their hair down. After the older guys go out a little bit, they're ready to go back home to their families 'cause they know what life's all about. We're family.

Robert "Wolfman" Belfour
(Red Banks, Mississippi)

There's just something about playing in a juke joint. I guess because I come up playing in some of these open houses, you know, we called them juke joints. You know, you go there and play all night [laughs]. So, it kind of relates back to that—when I was younger. I have a lot of fans who come to see me [at Red's]. But, you know, people have asked me, "Robert, why you play like you do? Why you make people feel like they do?" I say, "What do you mean? I just play what I feel." I didn't come up no hard way. I just worked on the farm as a kid. My mother sharecropped. And we had a few hard times, but it wasn't bad. To me, it wasn't as bad as some of the times I'm going through right now, you know, now that I got grown [laughs].

Louis "Gearshifter" Youngblood
(Jackson, Mississippi)

The Subway Lounge was a hotel at first—called the Summers Hotel, that I remember. And it had a little club kind of like beneath it. It was kind of like in the ground, like waist down, probably deeper than that 'cause you could look out the window, but you'd be looking at the sidewalk. It was a blues club. Always have been a blues club. Jimmy King had it, and they had a band in there. It had two doors you could go in and out, but when it was just a club, there wasn't but one way in and one way out. I didn't really like that. After Jimmy got it, customers still only used that one entrance, but there was another way out. The band used it. I don't know if the Subway was dangerous or not, but I believe it was [laughs]. And nobody thought about how dangerous it was. Man, that thing would be so full and packed you couldn't move without stepping on somebody's feet. You step on somebody's feet, you say, "Hey, I'm sorry." "Come on through." It was mostly young people. It was popular clear up to the end, even when it was falling down. The building was literally falling. The hotel part had done fell off [laughs]. It was through, but that little place was still there, and it was still jammed pack. They had this group called the Houserockers. Another thing, there were two clubs that would start at twelve o'clock. To me, I don't understand how they start at midnight, but that's what they did. They start at 12:00 and go 'til 3:30.

Red Paden

Red's is a juke joint. Just a place to have. It's just for guys our age. Someone has to keep a place for us to go. We can't really play around the house because people in the community complain about the music. They'll complain about anything. Guys like to come out and get away from the house. You can kind of raise your voice a little bit out there in the club. We still kind of give you that kind of atmosphere.

Wesley "Junebug" Jefferson (Clarksdale, Mississippi)

Red's gives me the feel all the blues that's been there. It gives me a feel of the blues more than a new place. A juke joint doesn't have any special rules much like a club would. You go in a juke joint and you might sit on the floor or move a chair over in the corner, and you can't do that in a club. And sometimes you might hear some language you don't want to hear. And sometimes every now and then a little corn liquor might get passed around. The only thing that's missing is the wood stove and the fish. You smell the fish, and you're in a juke joint then. You can go back to the cave days and they had some little stomping ground, so it's a traditional thing. Some people want to hear something that's way back there. They are really interested in that. They know about the other stuff. They just want to pick up what they can get from way back there, you know. Something they didn't know about.

Deejay Steve Ladd (Clarksdale, Mississippi)

Walking into Red's for the first time reminds me of back in the early '50s and what they'd call cafés up on that Texas-Oklahoma state line, where I'm from. A café there would have been a juke joint in the Delta. They had no license to do anything. You had chilidogs, catfish and pigs' feet. You could come in there, get a meal and drink your beer. There was no real stage, just a platform. Guys would just sit up there. One amplifier, one microphone and a drummer—and it was on. Juke joints were average occupancy of forty or fifty, and you got one hundred in there. People stepping on your toes, "'Scuse me." No fire code [laughs]. Here it is a new millennium, and it's still got that 1940s, '50s flavor in there. There's not going to be no waxed floor. It's dark. To get that real blues flavor, it's definitely up in there. It's like Sarah's Kitchen, it's in there.

RED PADEN

It is a good thing that we still have teachers out there, but we have very few that are willing to listen to the past. I think the only way you can make it in the future is if you know about the past. You know about the mistakes that we've made and the times we went through. And that's what's going to make you excel in the future. We used to play a lot of that downhome blues, but nowadays things have changed to where most of the blacks don't want to listen to that. It's a new generation now. I think we're going through a period of changes. That's why we keep the place down there—Red's Lounge. So we can remember the past.

JUKE OWNER "MISS" SARAH MOORE (CLARKSDALE, MISSISSIPPI)

It was called Crossroads Blues Club & Sarah's Kitchen. I moved from down there to here in '96 to open this Sarah's Kitchen. You know how it is. You done stayed up that Friday night, and you look like you ain't been to bed. And when the music starts, it just lifts you up. You know what I'm saying? I said, "Ooh, it sounds like a Saturday night juke house up in here." And I love the people. They really help me. I thank God for it. That is very important. I'm not doing it for the money. I just do it for the peoples. I just love 'em. I get all kinds of people from all over the world, and I tell them all the time when you get here you're my people now. You're at home, you know. You're welcome here. You can't get the big head. You can't get greedy and want to try to make all the money. You got to let somebody else make some. It weren't meant for me to make it all.

Josh "Razorblade" Stewart (Clarksdale, Mississippi)

In a juke joint, you see smoke everywhere, you can't hardly see who's playing or who's singing, but you hearing all this good music coming from the soul. It's coming from the heart. Sarah is a nice, easy-going lady. She likes pleasing people. She don't open to really make no money, but this is what she loves doing. To me, Sarah's Kitchen is like a juke joint because it's got that kind of feel. And look man, from right here at Sarah's Kitchen, you don't know who you'll meet or where you'll go. The main reason we're down at Sarah's is to work with the kids to let them see what it feels like to perform before a "live" audience, so they won't feel like the audience is jumping out at them. It's a training thing, a learning experience. You've got to always be humble in this business. It's a dirty business, but you got to learn how to deal with it. You got to take the bitter with the sweet and go head on. I try not to let it worry me, but it do sometimes. Most of the stuff I write about are life situations that really happened to me at one time or another, and I'm sure that I'm not the only one they've happened to. Like me as a young musician, I played like these youngsters today, but Monday morning I had to go meet that mule, so it was always really more of a hobby. I just done got too old to hold down a job, and this was always my first love, whether I had a job or not. If I never get rich and famous, it ain't going to make me no difference. I just want to be remembered as a good musician from Clarksdale who maybe tried to help some of the young ones.

"Big" Jack Johnson (Clarksdale, Mississippi)

I met Frank Frost and Sam Carr in 1962 at the Savoy Theater, down by the railroad tracks in Clarksdale. It was a movie theater, like the New Roxy. There used to be about three or four movie theaters here. Clarksdale used to be the place. Everybody would try to come here. We got together down there one Saturday night in 1962 and stayed together thirty-five years. We played after the movie. Shoot, man. It wasn't like it is now. Back then, the plantations were running Clarksdale. Only they'd say "when," so the music ran all night long.

Mary Ann "Action" Jackson
(Senatobia, Mississippi)

I lived out in the fields on the plantation of Rosebud Farm. My mother had eleven children. I was a little girl picking cotton, piling it up in the middle of the field. My sister would come along and put it in the bag 'cause I couldn't pick it up. We had mules and wagons, but your tractors came on after that. There weren't but one or two tractors. There weren't any blues players in my family, but I used to go out to the little juke joints and hear music and stuff playing out there. It wasn't nothing but toe tappin' and foot stompin' and finger poppin' and all that [laughs]. Uh huh. I can remember juke joints like the Blue Flame Café. That was out on Highway Number 4. And, well, all the ones that were there, they've torn them all down. It's been so long ago.

John Horton

My father played guitar. He'd put that slide on it and go to work. We used to be out with him 'til about seven o'clock in the morning when we were about six or seven years old. They'd gather at them juke houses, get their little cooking together and he'd pull out his guitar. Boy, they'd never get enough. I mean, they'd party all night. Yes sir. 'Til about seven the next day. That was blues. What I tell a lot of people now, back in them days if it's just a one piece or whatever, it was real exciting because that was it. Wasn't no pop hits. Wasn't none of that. Just straight out blues. When we were little kids, if we saw a guy by himself—one of them old-timers—we thought that was as exciting as it could be, man.

Terry "Harmonica" Bean

There was twenty-four of us in the family in all, and my father and grandfather played blues. I was the only one that carried the blues on. My daddy played the electric band style of guitar, but my grandfather played the old acoustic. My mother left me when I was a year old, and my father raised me. When I would go down to my mother's house, my grandfather would get the old acoustic guitar from under the bed and play one-man style. I liked that, and a lot of that stuff that I do now is from that stuff that he was doing. His name was Rossie Johnson. He passed away in '82. I was playing around then, but what got me away from guitar playing for a while was that my daddy and them would go in these juke joints. Back at that time, there was juke joints everywhere and house parties. My daddy was a big gambler, so he'd put us all in the car, and he'd go gamble at these people's houses. Before the night's over, they'd all get their guitars out and go to playing, and they'd call me in to play 'cause my daddy knew that I could do it. Then my other brothers got kind of upset by me getting all the attention like that, and they would jump on me when my daddy wasn't around. So, I quit playing and started playing baseball. I was almost drafted into the major leagues for baseball. In 1980, I was going to be drafted by the Kansas City Royals, Cincinnati Reds or either California Angels as a pitcher. I threw with both hands, about ninety-five, ninety-six [miles per hour]. I had a motorcycle wreck in '80, and it cost me that major-league career. That's when I started doing blues professionally.

Jimmy "Duck" Holmes (Bentonia, Mississippi)

They didn't have no amplifier. No microphone. They played juke joints. There was nothing to help people's voice out too much, so you got five or ten people in a little ole small room, you got to make them hear what you're saying. You got to sing and holler. Over a period of time, they got adjusted to that. That's why they sing that loud pitch. Real loud. Now, I've played as hard with nobody in here as when the place was packed. Jack [Owens] would do the same thing and Henry Stuckey. You could hear him some nights. He be at home sitting on his porch just playing away. Jack was

Jimmy "Duck" Holmes on the airport tarmac on his way to Geneva, Switzerland, with "Harmonica" Bean and "Gearshifter." *Lou Bopp.*

Jackson, Mississippi bluesman Louis "Gearshifter" Youngblood loves the comfortable atmosphere that juke joints offer. *Lou Bopp.*

the same way. He would get his guitar out and play just as hard as if he thought he was singing to an audience. I guess that's the blues part about it. Playing guitar and singing will lift you back up. That's something they had in common. They played just as hard around home.

LOUIS "GEARSHIFTER" YOUNGBLOOD

I played places around Jackson and on Farrish. Farrish Street was similar to what? To Bourbon or Beale Street, at night. In the daytime, it was just a street you'd go down. They had little ole restaurant or something, at least one in every block. Juke joints were up and down Farrish. And the majority would have some kind of entertainment at night. Blues. That's what they played in Mississippi until this disco came in. When this disco came in, it changed a lot. For a minute there, they were saying, "The blues is through." No, the blues ain't through. It might be taking a break, but it ain't through. It took a minute. Today, it's like we're losing blues again to a certain extent. It's like we're losing it again in a way, but this time it ain't just being renamed. It's kind of just fading out 'cause of a lack of interest. I don't know, I ain't as young as I used to be. There's a few under me. But after those are through, I don't know how wide the variety going to be after that. There are only a few old guys. The majority ain't here no more. The blues audience? The ones that haven't gone to the church have probably gone to hell! [Laughs.] *My great-grandmother used to tell me that if I wasn't singing gospel, then I was singing blues. No, I don't think it's what you sing, I think it's what's in the heart. 'Cause like, a lot of people say things, but do you actually mean it? Or do you put it in motion and follow through? I hear some people say it's who you let see you do it. But I say it's the mind of the person that's doing it. There are some things you don't do. If you want to go places, there's a way to go. You can't just go how you want to go. You might have to get with the program. I figured out if blues carried me to places that I have never been, fed me and clothed me, then there was something more to it than anybody let you know. The blues carry me to places that I never even thought about.*

MOONSHINE AKA WHITE WHISKEY

A few years back, I hosted a book signing for a fellow History Press author at my Cat Head blues store. It was during Juke Joint Festival week in Clarksdale, so thousands of music fans from all around the world were wandering around our historic little blues town.

The book was called *Mississippi Moonshine Politics*, so I thought, "Hmm, what would make the signing even more memorable for tourists? Free moonshine samples, of course." Brilliant, I know.

I still had one jar of 'shine left over from a recent documentary filming. The moonshiner himself had since passed away, after a life of smoking, but his potent product lived on—if only in one jar. (More on the old man later.)

I dropped by the grocery, picked up some small plastic cups, set up a little counter display next to the book-signing table and proceeded to go about my busy festival weekend. In my marketing brilliance, it honestly hadn't occurred to me that such a book might attract not only tourists but also those "in the business"—not moonshiners, but what "Machine Gun" Kelly once labeled "G-Men" (aka government men).

Sure enough, unbeknownst to me at the time, three such G-men got their books signed on that festive Saturday at Cat Head—apparently marveling at the high quality of the refreshing samples in question.

First thing that Monday morning, a well-chiseled, well-dressed man with a badge walked right out of central casting and into my store. He peppered me with questions as my knees weakened. Since both the evidence and the manufacturer were gone (drunk up and buried down,

Sometimes beer is just not enough for juke joint partiers. (And sometimes what it says on the label isn't what's found inside.) *Lou Bopp.*

respectively), I felt less than verbose. After all, loose lips sink ships or juke joints or something.

I share this anecdote to illustrate the simple fact that many visitors to the Magnolia State don't seem to realize that moonshine is now, and has always been, illegal. The stated reason usually involves "health and safety," which certainly has its merits, but in the end, like many things in life, it mostly comes down to taxes—or a lack thereof.

Hence, moonshine is actually pretty rare these days—only showing up once in a blue moon, usually at a juke or house party, usually as a quick swig from the pocket of a nameless local partygoer. Personally, I think it's part of the Mississippi blues experience, but please proceed at your own risk. Oh, and please burn this chapter after reading.

Baptised on Muddy Waters...or Moonshine

As I recall in more detail in my last book, I first sampled moonshine from a repurposed milk jug at Junior Kimbrough's old country juke joint in Chulahoma, Mississippi. It tasted vaguely of corn and plastic. It definitely took the edge off, resulting in plenty of relaxed smiles and loose dancing as local favorites like R.L. Burnside and Kimbrough grooved on 'til the early morning hours.

Junior's son Robert Kimbrough Sr., told me a decade later:

> *Moonshine is just a tradition in Mississippi. If you knew R.L. Burnside, then you know about the moonshine—'cause that fellow kept it. My dad, he kept moonshine and also that homebrew in the quart bottles. They would get drunk off of that. It was like wine, and it was good. But that moonshine? It was tradition, man. It was there all the time. All the time* [laughs].

Moonshine, of course, is nothing new to the blues, as Robert Johnson's partner David "Honeyboy" Edwards explained to me when he was ninety years old:

> *At that time, a lot of peoples in the country would have dances, and there was a lot of people in the country making white whiskey. That's how they made their living. Other bootleggers would come in and buy three or four gallons. Just like if I was a distributor, I made whiskey at my house—twenty-five, thirty gallons a night. If you're a bootlegger, you'd come by and get two gallons from me for three dollars a gallon. I'm making money 'cause I'm making about fifteen, twenty gallon. I ain't selling by no drinks. I'm just selling by the gallon. And the bootlegger, he get it from me and distributes, selling by the drink, selling by the pint. He makes his money like that. But I ain't got time. I'm making too much money selling by the gallon. You know what I mean?*

Of course, juke joints and whiskey had their risks back then, as Tom Graves reminded us in *Crossroads: The Life and Afterlife of Blues Legend Robert Johnson*: "The tale most often told about how Johnson met his fate is that he was poisoned by a jealous husband who put strychnine in his whiskey. As the story goes, Johnson was booked to play a rural juke joint just outside Greenwood, Mississippi, that Honeyboy Edwards recalled was named Three Forks. Johnson apparently had struck up an ill-considered affair with the juke joint operator's wife."

Nevertheless, eight-plus decades later, whiskey and jukes are still part of the blues life here. Perhaps part of the reason why Mississippi's taste for moonshine has survived into twenty-first century is that while national Prohibition in the United States lasted "only" from 1920 to 1933 (giving

Clarksdale, Mississippi's Anthony "Big A" Sherrod plays juke joint blues as bassist "Jabbo" looks on. *Lou Bopp.*

A fire pit burns while the blues plays at the New Roxy in Clarksdale's historic New World District. *Lou Bopp.*

Local partygoers search for faces they know on the walls of Mississippi's oldest juke, Bentonia's Blue Front Café. *Lou Bopp*.

Blues history on top of blues history. The sign up top says LaVene Music Center. The sign below says Red's. *Lou Bopp*.

Perhaps the last rural juke joint, Po Monkey's Lounge was surrounded by cotton fields with plenty of dirt road parking. *Lou Bopp.*

Although the structure was clearly built without the aid of an architect (or code enforcement), Willie "Po Monkey" Seaberry ran his juke for more than fifty years. *Lou Bopp.*

Most Mississippi Delta towns were once awash in cotton money. Today, many can't even sustain blues clubs. *Lou Bopp.*

Do Drop Inn's owner, Arnold Lopez, runs the former "live" music juke joint mostly as a regular bar these days. *Lou Bopp.*

Bentonia, Mississippi's long-running Blue Front juke joint features sporadic music but still caters to local customers daily. *Lou Bopp.*

Louis "Gearshifter" Youngblood learned blues from his father and grandmother. Here he performs in the *We Juke Up in Here!* film. *Lou Bopp.*

Local soul blues band performs at Bentonia's Blue Front Café for the *We Juke Up in Here!* documentary. *Lou Bopp.*

Described as the "torchbearer for Clarksdale blues," Anthony "Big A" Sherrod started playing juke joints as a preteen. *Lou Bopp.*

Clarksdale's Annie Bell's Lounge (attached to a recently closed all-night burger joint) only books deejays nowadays. *Lou Bopp.*

Juke joint proprietor Willie "Po Monkey" Seaberry, standing in the cotton field he worked, dressed for his blues party night. *Lou Bopp.*

Thousands of blues lovers, partygoers and (later) tourists walked up the rickety stairs to Po Monkey's good time joint. *Lou Bopp.*

Late-in-life gospel/blues discovery Leo "Bud" Welch was as comfortable at a yard party as a juke joint—or even a church. *Lou Bopp.*

Musician Leo "Bud" Welch shines on after filming an episode for the *Moonshine & Mojo Hands* blues series. *Lou Bopp.*

DJ Hype's juke joint was inside an old gas station in Clarksdale and featured both deejays and occasional blues bands. *Lou Bopp.*

Some moonshiners come up with their own recipes and modifications to Mississippi's favorite illicit beverage. *Lou Bopp.*

The age of Mississippi sharecropping may be over, but cotton chopping has returned as pigweed has become resistant to herbicides. *Lou Bopp.*

Musician Josh "Razorblade" Stewart jumped out of airplanes in Vietnam before returning to Clarksdale to sing the blues. *Lou Bopp.*

Before opening his own juke joint, bluesman Robert "Bilbo" Walker was a regular performer at Red's Lounge in Clarksdale. *Lou Bopp.*

Moonshine and barbecued raccoon are as at home at a North Mississippi Hill Country yard party as the blues music being played. *Lou Bopp.*

Many of Clarksdale's blues bands feature young players; here "Kingfish" and "Hollywood" prepare to back Lucious Spiller. *Lou Bopp.*

Right: Bluesman Lucious Spiller has family roots in Grenada, Mississippi, but moved to Clarksdale in 2017 from Little Rock. *Lou Bopp.*

Below: The late Riverside Hotel owner, Frank "Rat" Ratliff, could rattle off dozens of famous blues players who stayed at his place. *Lou Bopp.*

Located on what was historically the African American side of the railroad tracks, the renovated New Roxy is a favorite musical hangout. *Lou Bopp.*

Club 2000 owner Nancy Saffold once employed a barman who opened the beers with his teeth. (He didn't last long.) *Lou Bopp.*

Andre "Otha" Evans and friends demonstrate a fife-and-drum style once played by blues elders Otha Turner and Napoleon Strickland. *Lou Bopp.*

The late "Mr. Johnnie" Billington taught young kids from tough neighborhoods to play the blues in jukes across the Delta. *Lou Bopp.*

Clarksdale bluesman Terry "Big T" Williams ran four different juke joints at various times—when he wasn't out fishing. *Lou Bopp.*

It may look like Mississippi, but "Harmonica" Bean and "Duck" Holmes are actually playing in Old Town Geneva, Switzerland. *Lou Bopp.*

rise to gangsters like Al "Scarface" Capone along the way), Mississippi's liquor prohibition (which actually started in 1908) didn't end until one-term governor Paul B. Johnson, one might say, decided that his own bourbon drinking necessitated such a change in 1966.

Amazingly, Mississippi's first legal post-prohibition liquor store, the Jigger & Jug in Greenville, didn't open until that year. Even today, liquor sales are not technically legal statewide. What is legal is for each town or municipality to make its own decisions regarding alcohol, locally. Then that legal status and the actual wholesale liquor sales are controlled by the state. To that end, the Mississippi Tax Commission set up the Office of Alcohol Beverage Control (ABC), and the rest is history. Sort of.

Since Mississippi still has a taste for the hard stuff, and several "dry counties" continue on with various levels of prohibition, a lot of party people still take a shine to their favorite blues beverage.

A Visit with an Old Moonshiner

In 2013, my filmmaking co-producer Jeff Konkel and I interviewed an old moonshiner for our appropriately titled travel series *Moonshine & Mojo Hands* on what turned out to be the eve of his passing.

One could say that he was more of a hobbyist than a businessman when it came to the illicit hooch since he preferred to give it away to friends and family rather than sell it to strangers. Still, he was a real-deal 'shiner who had refined his process and product for decades, distilling it down to near store-bought quality—despite his very DIY setup and drafty old barn workspace.

To our mystery moonshiner in Somewhere, Mississippi, distilling white whiskey was part of both his own upbringing and the blues culture he loved so much:

> *I've been around moonshine all my life. My dad made moonshine. And all the stories of hearing mom talk about dad, and my brother talking about delivering the moonshine and everything, I just decided I needed some. When people from all over the world come to the Delta, one of the things that they like knowing is that they have sampled some moonshine, 'cause that's on their bucket list when they're coming to the Delta and experiencing the blues.*

As for the secret to his success, he talked science and said it had everything to do with consistency:

> *What it is. You have steam rising, which is alcohol vapor. And it runs into that coil. This is real hot. And when it hits the water, those vapors turn back into a liquid, and that what runs out. You have obviously spent a lot of time mastering this process and figuring out the quality control to get the highest possible quality. This is the simple part. Anybody can do this. Anybody can run it and get a product out of there. But it takes some time, and it takes some documenting, so you can go back to look at what worked and what didn't work here. [I worked to make it] consistent. Every time I run it, it's going to be the same. I do my cuts and everything the same every time.*

Moonshine and the Bluesman

Another blues character I used to know was both a professional musician and self-taught moonshiner. (Of course, if a jar of his 'shine sat long enough, you'd see a bit of strange sediment at the bottom of the jar, so my advice was always, "Drink up!" and quickly.)

The same gentleman also raised a lot of his own food. I ran into him once at a hole-in-the-wall joint in the Delta, and after shaking hands and talking for a minute, he said, "Oh man, I've got something for you out in the truck." I'm thinking moonshine, but in fact, it was a big chunk of "homemade" bacon. He smacked the naked chunk of bacon onto the naked wooden bar table (that was possibly cleaned at some point in history) and proceeded to tell me exactly how one goes about making bacon, all the while poking it with his index finger. Now, anyone who knows me knows I'm a hand-sanitizer man. I order my burger well done, and I smell the carton of milk when I pull it out of the fridge. So, as nice as the bluesman-moonshiner was to share his big hunk of bacon with me, the whole time he's talking, I'm thinking, "There are so many reasons why that pig part will never cross my lips."

The point of the story? In Mississippi, making bacon and making moonshine are both just part of a homegrown culture that comes from a countryside once filled with shacks, sharecroppers and juke joints.

House parties, yard parties and juke joints are natural places for both bluesmen and moonshine to put on a show. *Lou Bopp.*

Making something out of nearly nothing is as natural here as mosquitoes and blues fans.

Time for a Classic "Moonshine Run"

As evidenced here, I've met some incredible blues characters since I first started visiting Mississippi in the mid-1990s. If you read about them in a novel, you'd as likely roll your eyes as crack a smile. Again, I hesitate to use real names here. Pardon me if I err on the side of caution, but trust me, I'm not exaggerating. Not even a little bit.

My buddy Konkel and I have visited a particular Mississippi bluesman several times over the years to attend his quasi-regular, house and yard parties. I'll call the musician "Mr. Man" to protect his identity

One particular Sunday afternoon, Konkel and I were listening to Mr. Man crank out his grooving blues with a ragtag, makeshift band in the side yard. His wife served barbecued pork steaks from the kitchen, and soon after, we tossed our empty paper plates into a growing pile of trash. About that time, another woman came flying out the front screen door yelling, "Don't eat the meat! Don't eat the meat! It's got worms in it!" Too late. We had, in fact, eaten the meat.

Since there were apparently no stomach pumps on hand, we took alternate emergency measures. We headed out in a well-used car with a crooked steering wheel and a questionable tour guide in search of more alcohol for the party. (My van was blocked in by our more recent party arrivals.) Of course, a dry county on a Sunday afternoon meant that we'd have to resort to old-school means of securing the appropriate libations.

At the first house we visited, I apparently jumped out of borrowed car too quickly and enthusiastically. I was suspected of being a "revenue man," leading the moonshine purveyor to insist that he knew nothing about nothing.

Our tour guide informed me that I was to remain slow and silent for our next stop, which proved infinitely more successful as a result. Upon our return, a mildly intoxicated man holding a twenty-four-ounce "tall boy" drove into the yard. He was driving one of those short school buses and wanted to show us the 1970s-era home stereo he'd installed inside. We weren't sure what comment he was seeking from us, but we agreed that it was "pretty darn cool" and unlike any school bus we ridden in as kids.

Next up, two hard-looking, shirtless black men riding bareback on horses inexplicably rambled into the yard, seemingly from nowhere. They were rough-riding cowboys who lived off the land but still appreciated a good blues jam.

As the sun slowly set, a cold wind began to blow, threatening the yard party vibe. Fortunately, one of the nameless neighbors leaped into action, grabbing a couple of old tires from the bushes, a can of lighter fluid and a match.

I'd grown up watching 1970s nightly news filled with tire fires in far-off places like Beirut. But I'd never actually witnessed one firsthand. Two observations: first, they burn incredibly hot (it felt good); second, they burn up completely (makes for easy cleanup). Still, the ultra-thick black smoke was breathtaking—literally.

We just kept trying to appear sober and reasonable as we prepared our official stories for the police and firemen who would surely be arriving in short order. But to our surprise, the only folks who arrived were more blues partygoers, attracted like moths to a flame.

Apparently, this was not an unusual sight (or stench) in Mr. Man's neighborhood. Or perhaps local law enforcement was a bit frightened by the general chaos?

Traditional blues dancers are often fueled by Mississippi's favorite juke joint beverage. *Lou Bopp.*

As the tires slowly became black spots on the scorched earth, Konkel and I tried to fuel the cause, pulling old cardboard boxes from the back of my '99 Dodge van. Honestly, we thought we were the smart ones. After all, who in the heck burns car tires when you have completely reasonable cardboard boxes to flame up? Soon, glowing cardboard embers were rising from the heat and landing in nearby trees and on Mr. Man's house. It was time for us to go.

A Homemade Juke Joint and More 'Shine

Someone in the evening's haze suggested that we visit an unadvertised juke joint in the neighboring countryside, so off into the night we drove with a designated-driver friend, reeking of burnt rubber and undercooked pork.

The ancient owner was wearing a holster filled with cold hard steel, which was fortunately softened by his seemingly permanent smile. He offered us free beers (apparently a courtesy to first-time, out-of-town guests), and I noticed that as he opened and closed the fridge, there were at least a dozen recycled pint bottles full of moonshine in the lettuce crisper.

There wasn't music that first night, so we returned later to hear "live" blues. But regardless, the visit was as solid a Mississippi blues experience as you can have. Actually, the whole afternoon and evening qualified as unforgettable—steeped in blues and moonshine, as they were.

Mississippi is like an onion. It's made up of layers. Some good, some otherwise, but all are fascinating. And the music here is always amazing. It comes brandishing a smile, a bottle and sometimes even a pistol.

THE DEATH OF PO MONKEY'S

When seventy-four-year-old field worker, party animal and juke joint runner Willie Seaberry passed away unexpectedly in July 2016, an era in Mississippi blues culture passed with him. The colorful character known to his friends and fans as simply "Po Monkey" was the last man standing. He and his country juke—which were essentially one and the same—came from a time and place that had long since moved on everywhere else. But somehow, someway, Seaberry kept the tradition going sixteen years into the new millennium.

The tradition of a weekly blues house party (note that Seaberry actually lived in a small room off to the side of the main party space) on the cotton farms of Mississippi reaches far back in history to just after the Civil War. Seaberry once told me that his personal history with running such a house party or juke joint out of the former-sharecropper's shack reached back to 1963.

Run first as a mostly private party and later becoming more and more public, by the end of the juke's lengthy run, it had been featured in many high-profile photography books (e.g., Annie Leibovitz), travel books (e.g., *Dispatches from Pluto*), newspapers (e.g.. the *New York Times*), cable TV series (e.g., Anthony Bourdain), network TV shows (e.g., *Good Morning America*) and documentary films (e.g., *We Juke Up in Here!*). In the end, you were as likely to see young college kids or famous rock stars as you were African American locals on Thursday's weekly "family night." But like

Willie Seaberry, proprietor and resident of the sharecropper shack turned juke joint Po Monkey's Lounge. *Lou Bopp.*

Po Monkey's owner, Willie Seaberry, was known for his colorful late-night suits and (often) even more colorful props and signs. *Lou Bopp.*

other older juke runners, Seaberry still ran the place his way. An air of authenticity always pervaded the creaky old structure. It remained the real deal.

Po Monkey's Before Blues Tourism

On the night of Thursday, July 14, 2016, I got a text from a friend. "Po Monkey died." Hoping that it wasn't true, I searched my phone for the legendary juke runner's phone number. I plugged in "Monkey," and because I live in the surreal world of Mississippi blues, three entries came up (including one for the "Monkeys Riding Dogs" we book for our Juke Joint Festival in Clarksdale each April).

As it turned out, Mr. Seaberry had indeed passed away. According to newspaper accounts that weekend, he had a heart attack while in his bed at the juke, perhaps a day or two before they found him.

Apparently, folks had started to show up for Seaberry's weekly Thursday night blues deejay party (including the deejay), but the juke was locked up tight. Since this had never happened before, eventually someone broke in to check on the proprietor, only to find he had passed on to the big juke house in the sky.

Twenty years before this fateful passing, I first passed through the doors of Po Monkey's Lounge, after receiving some very convoluted directions from locals that first put me in the town of Merigold. Everyone said, "Monkey's place is in Merigold." In fact, it was a mile and a half off Highway 61—out in the countryside off a gravel road on an old Delta farm. I was still married then and living an ad man's life in St. Louis, Missouri, but fortunately my wife wasn't afraid of a little blues adventure.

Clearly built without the aid of an architect, the crazy structure known as Po Monkey's Lounge sat in the middle of a cotton field. As we walked in, the tall, smiling proprietor rushed over to greet us. He escorted us to a table and took our beer order. There was a deejay spinning soul-blues, and the crowd was entirely local and black—a mix of singles and couples, mostly middle aged. We sat down at a table, receiving nods from the fellow partiers sitting around us. Everyone was friendly, if keeping to themselves initially. (Later, after a few beverages, a young man gave me the recipe for raccoon roadkill baked with sweet potatoes—not sure how the conversation got there.)

The interior of Po Monkey's was decorated with colorful lights, beer ads and stuffed (sometimes enhanced) monkeys. *Lou Bopp.*

As Seaberry headed toward his makeshift bar to grab some oversized bottles of ice-cold Bud, we looked around, trying to get the lay of the land. That's when I realized the small, suspended TVs hanging near the ceiling (like the ones you used to see in hospital rooms) were all running the same... uh, programming. Yup. Turns out that Mr. Seaberry was a fan of the adult film industry. His TVs were all synced together and playing as graphic a video as you can imagine.

Now, I'm far from being a prude, but honestly, one does not expect to encounter such bachelor party content in a public setting, sitting among other members of civilized society. I guess my face—ok, our faces—showed it.

Seaberry caught our reaction, spun back around from the bar, rushed back to our table, leaned in and said, "Now, I can cut that off, if it's bothering y'all." I'm sure my face turned beet red as I laughed and said something like, "I'm not going to be the guy who walks into your party and tells you to shut it down!"

That's what Po Monkey's was—a party place. It was that juke joint meets house party hybrid that some might call a jukehouse. Mr. Seaberry lived there, worked there and partied there. It was his world, his rules. Every Thursday night, the gracious host essentially invited friends and strangers alike into his living room. And what a living room is was. I won't repeat everything I saw there through the years, but let's just say that the man knew how to have a good time.

Tourism Brings "Live" Music, New Audience

After I moved to the Mississippi Delta in 2002, I met Luther Brown, a professor at Delta State University in Cleveland, Mississippi. He and another professor, Henry Outlaw, along with their academic team, befriended Willie Seaberry. Since Cleveland didn't really have much of a blues club culture, and Po Monkey's Lounge was only ten minutes north on Highway 61, Delta State's Delta Center for Culture & Learning began booking occasional "live" blues shows at the old juke on nights other than Thursday.

Brown would call me and say he had some donated funds to work with, and I would book or recommend a blues act to play the party. Over the decade that followed, I helped put a true who's who of modern Delta blues legends into the tiny deejay corner of Po Monkey's. Since it was never designed to hold a full band, there were some hilarious nights were trios and quartets were nearly piled up on one another, trying to stay out of the way of the packed audience that frankly had nowhere to fit either.

Some of my favorites who played those unforgettable evenings include Terry "Harmonica" Bean, Jimmy "Duck" Holmes, James "T-Model" Ford, John Horton, "Cadillac" John Nolden, Bill Abel, Lightnin' Malcolm, All Night Long Blues Band, Terry "Big T" Williams, Wesley "Junebug" Jefferson, Robert "Bilbo" Walker, Anthony "Big A" Sherrod and Walter "Mississippi Slim" Horn.

I also booked in "Big" George Brock one time. In fact, that night perfectly illustrates the evolution of Po Monkey's from a local party to a tourism phenomenon.

I had just released a comeback album on Brock and had him playing at the King Biscuit Blues Festival in nearby Helena, Arkansas. (I also had Brock working that week with judo/bluesman/wannabe actor Steven Seagal, who was recording an all-star "blues album" up in Memphis. But that's a whole other story.)

Whereas my first 1990s visit to Po Monkey's featured a local African American audience, soul-blues deejay and adult movies, after the local university started facilitating "live" blues shows at the rural juke joint, both the complexion of the audience and the TV show content slowly evolved to accommodate the new money walking through the old door. By the time I booked Big George Brock there in 2005, there were as many tourists in the audience as locals, and classic *Seinfeld* reruns glowed silently on the television sets. What a difference a decade makes.

In 2009, I helped book the deep-blues trio of T-Model Ford, Terry "Harmonica" Bean and Lee Williams to play a Monkey's gig for *Good Morning America Weekend Edition*. Before the performance, *GMA* also wanted to interview T-Model. I tried in vain to suggest a few safe lines of questioning to the producer and on-camera interviewer, but they were from the big city and joyfully ignored me. As a result, if you saw the piece, you might have noticed that there wasn't more than five seconds of T-Model speaking—from his twenty-five-minute interview.

Let's just say that the interviewer began with an open-ended generic blues question, and T-Model immediately took it and ran with it—turning it into an explicit tale explaining his self-assigned nickname, "the Ladies' Man," in detail. Sitting nearby, the gentleman they called Po Monkey laughed to himself.

Po Monkey Jukes Up in There

Later, we filmed a short segment at Po Monkey's Lounge for our 2012 juke joint documentary *We Juke Up in Here!*

The production team—Jeff Konkel, Damien Blaylock, Lou Bopp and yours truly—arrived just prior to sunset to film Seaberry out front of his juke. When we arrived, he was standing out in the plowed rows of rich Delta soil surrounding his place, smoking a big dirty cigar in a clean pair of overalls.

Always on a ridiculously low budget, Jeff and I really wanted some rolling shots inside the iconic building. Blaylock suggested using a wheelchair as a dolly of sorts, so I rented one the day before from a drugstore just down the street from Cat Head. Seaberry looked at us like we were total idiots (which was certainly possible), rolling camera-bearing Blaylock around inside his very tight and crooked-floored joint for twenty minutes. But to his credit, he was patient and accommodating as we rolled the camera to within inches of his long cigar as he tried in vain to watch TV, waiting for us to be done and some cash to be placed in his large weathered hands.

In the end, it was a sweet segment—one that stands as a short tribute to this tall tale of a man and his party-on mission.

Until his sun finally set, Po Monkey's owner, Willie Seaberry, worked the cotton fields surrounding his juke. *Lou Bopp.*

And Now, the End Is Near...

Even in death, Willie "Po Monkey" Seaberry did it his way as the final curtain closed.

The morning after authorities confirmed his passing, one of Seaberry's longtime friends dropped by my store to make sure that I'd heard that the party was over.

Larry Grimes is a Vietnam vet, a former Parchman Prison guard and a bit of a juke joint character himself. A funny, grinning white guy seemingly from another planet but actually merely Rome, Mississippi, Grimes was the crafty character who made dozens of humorous signs, props and gags for Seaberry through the years. If you ever made it to Po Monkey's, sometime after 11:00 p.m., if he wasn't too tired from driving a tractor, Seaberry would come out from behind the bar and parade around his packed house. Usually, he would be wearing one of his colorful zoot suits, and often he would have something hanging from around his neck. Something to make you smile. Sometimes it was a two-sided sign that would have the start of a joke on one side and the often very adult punchline on the back. Other times, he would be wearing or holding a prop—a visual gag—that from an adult or in some other way "non-PC" perspective was designed to make you laugh. And laugh you would, no matter what. That was the unwritten rule.

Grimes and I reminisced for a few minutes, and then he got to the gossip. "You know, most folks don't know that Monkey had a wife," he said. I confirmed that I had never heard about her and noted that he certainly didn't act like a man who was married.

He continued, saying something like, "Yeah, he wasn't really sure if they were still married, but I guess they were. Oh, and did I tell you he had a bunch of cash at the place? Most of it was in his truck. I knew about it, so I told [the authorities] to get it." Wow. What a character. Well, both of them, really.

Sure enough, at the funeral, his wife-from-the-past showed up, marriage certificate in hand, to prove to the locals and tourists alike that whatever was Po Monkey's would soon be hers.

After news reports of lawyers and rumors of DNA tests, his wife and her side of the family were legally deemed the owners of everything at Po Monkey's Lounge except the building and the land, which was and still is owned by the farm.

House Parties, Hustlers & the Blues Life

Septuagenarian blues partier Seaberry looks back on his life's work—Po Monkey's Lounge, near Merigold, Mississippi. *Lou Bopp.*

For good measure, she apparently also trademarked the name "Po Monkey's Lounge," just in case anyone wanted to start making and selling branded merchandise.

As I was finishing this book, Seaberry's wife held an online auction to liquidate the juke's décor and fixtures, inside and out. While the ultimate fate of those artifacts is unknown as of this writing, there is definitely hope for a positive outcome for blues fans.

As opposed to a private collector buying the whole lot and entombing it in a basement somewhere, the Mississippi-based PORCH Society (Preservation of Rural Cultural and Heritage) nonprofit purchased everything. After the auction, PORCH founder Shonda Warner told the *Mississippi Business Journal* that she "wants to work with the Seaberry family, who stipulated that all of the items be kept together instead of being dispersed [risking] the loss of their identity, and also with the Hiter family on whose land the lounge and home are located…as 'a way to continue Willie's good work.'"

Good work, indeed.

THE JUKE JOINT HOTEL?

In music critic Robert Palmer's classic *Deep Blues*, he ends his book by asking the rhetorical question, "How much history can be communicated by pressure on a guitar string?" The same might be asked of a building—be it a juke joint or another deeply historic blues structure.

THE EMPRESS OF THE BLUES

Around 2005, an older, African American tourist came through my Cat Head store in Clarksdale. As is often the case, I struck up a conversation, asking where he was from, how long he planned to be in the area and so on. At some point, he mentioned a particular interest in Bessie Smith, the early, jazz-inflected blues singer from Tennessee who died in Clarksdale while on tour in the late 1930s. As the conversation continued, he began quoting from the original, racially charged legend surrounding her death—a legend first spread by record producer John Hammond Sr. via his 1937 *Down Beat* magazine article, "Did Bessie Smith Bleed to Death While Waiting for Medical Aid?"

In Hammond's version of events, told to him by a third party, Bessie Smith was turned away from a white hospital and died on the way to a black hospital in the Jim Crow days of the segregated South. A follow-up *Down Beat* article one month later largely corrected the story, but it was apparently too late, as the original version had already been absorbed into the public consciousness. Other media helped spread the story, and it even became the basis for a one-act play.

Thinking that my customer was interested in "the rest of the story," I set out to explain what I knew of the legend's origin, how it was spread and what we now know. Surprisingly, he became very agitated. Insisting that the legend was absolutely true, he abruptly left my store.

Old legends die hard, especially when they are steeped in a time when racial inequities in Mississippi were sadly the norm. Hammond's version of the story is certainly believable given the setting. To further complicate things, the Library of Congress's great field recordist Alan Lomax breathed new life into the old legend by repeating (and amplifying) Hammond's initial, unchecked version of the events in the otherwise excellent book *Land Where Blues Began* in 1993—more than half a century after Smith's untimely death.

As Lomax retold the tale:

> *Wounded in a local car wreck, the great blues singer was refused admission to three Clarksdale hospitals because she was black. In the end she bled to death without medical attention, while her friends pled with the hospital authorities to admit her. And this incident was typical of the Deep South.*

Bessie Smith: The Comeback Tour

On September 26, 1937, a somewhat past-her-prime African American singer was riding as the passenger in an older-model Packard cruising down Highway 61, just north of Clarksdale, Mississippi. It was after midnight, and the car was coming from Memphis, bound toward a concert in Rolling Fork. Called the "Empress of the Blues" during the highpoint of her fame in the 1920s, Bessie Smith's career had been in decline for some time. Although she hoped for a comeback, her hits were now more past than present.

Whereas the 1920s was the decade of the so-called Classic Blues Singers— bluesy female voices typically backed by jazz bands—the Great Depression decade of 1930s was more about the down-and-out male voices of the Deep South. The 1920s had kicked off with the first recorded "blues" song (actually more of a sentimental torch song than authentic blues), "Crazy Blues" by Mamie Smith (no relation to Bessie); her song was a tremendous hit that, according to the *Saturday Evening Post* years later, "sold for months at the rate of 7,500 copies a week." Soon after, Bessie eclipsed Mamie and her other competition in popularity, going on to become by many accounts the highest paid African American performer of the day. She recorded 160 sides total, mostly for Columbia Records.

   Sadly for Bessie Smith, by the early 1930s, that type of blues had faded. The Great Depression and the "talkies" (movies with synchronized sound) took a bite out of the recording market just as solo country bluesmen were hitting their stride with black southern audiences. Paramount Records, for example, sold more than ten thousand copies of some Charley Patton 78s just as the '20s were changing over to the '30s. Patton was an early star of Mississippi Delta blues and a much rougher, gutbucket type performer than any of the ladies in the Classic Blues era. Still, Smith was a star to many of her fans, and who knows what the future might have held for her? John Hammond Sr. himself had help record her final sides in 1933 and would certainly have included Smith in his groundbreaking "Spirituals to Swing" concerts at Carnegie Hall in 1938 and '39 had she survived. Perhaps a successful comeback was possible, but the world will never know.

Clarksdale, Mississippi—home of the legendary Riverside Hotel—was once the "Golden Buckle on the Cotton Belt." *Lou Bopp*.

CLARKSDALE, MISSISSIPPI, 1937

As Smith's car, piloted by her boyfriend, Richard Morgan (musician Lionel Hampton's uncle and not Smith's legal husband), drove south on Highway 61, they surely passed miles and miles of cotton, awaiting harvest in the clear, dark night. As they rode the two-lane highway toward the now mythical "crossroads" junction of 61 and 49, disaster struck a bit before 2:00 a.m. just north of Clarksdale, near the tiny town of Coahoma.

On October 3, 1957, almost exactly twenty years after that fateful night, Clarksdale's *Press Register* printed an investigation of the incident. Written by staff writer B.J. Skelton, most of the accident's details came from an August 27, 1957 letter by Dr. Hugh Smith, a white physician from Memphis who was on the scene the accident that night. (WROX Museum founder Bubba O'Keefe maintains these documents in his Clarksdale archive.)

Dr. Smith and a friend were the first to arrive on the Bessie Smith accident scene. The doctor reported:

> *We came upon an automobile, obviously a total wreck....We came to a stop some 30 feet from the automobile with my lights shining on a colored woman lying on the concrete road, obviously in serious condition....My associate and I jumped out of the car, and I examined the colored woman in the light of my headlights. Her left arm, at the elbow had been completely torn loose at the joint...in essence, a traumatic amputation except that the main artery was still intact.*

The doctor went on to relate the story told to him by Smith's driver. According to Morgan, their Packard had hit a large trailer truck that was slowly pulling back onto the road after an impromptu tire check by the truck's driver. The Packard hit the truck, nearly going beneath it and completely shearing off the car's wooden top before turning over and apparently ejecting passengers Morgan and Smith. The truck driver stated that he was carrying both U.S. mail and the Sunday morning edition of Memphis's *Commercial Appeal* newspaper and therefore "had" to leave the scene of the accident. He promised to send an ambulance from Clarksdale.

Dr. Smith applied a tourniquet to Bessie Smith's severed arm and sent his partner to a nearby farmhouse to ensure that an ambulance was indeed on its way. After several minutes had elapsed, the doctor began to clear out the back of his brand-new Chevrolet with plans to carry the gravely injured singer to Clarksdale himself. Suddenly, in the distance, a fast-moving car could be heard. The doctor attempted to signal the other driver by flashing his lights, but the car was still traveling at full speed when it slammed into the back of the Chevy, carrying it into the already wrecked Packard. Finally, with now three wrecked automobiles and at least three injured parties on the side of the road, two ambulances arrived on the scene.

The next day, the doctor noted:

> *Before I left Clarksdale, I, by chance, ran into the ambulance driver and inquired as to Bessie Smith's condition. He advised me that she had been taken either to a Negro clinic or a Negro hospital and expired several hours after arriving.*

Press Register reporter B.J. Skelton followed up on this for his 1957 article:

> *The ambulance driver* [Willie George Miller] *was located and asked about his recollection of the accident....Miller, although confessing that his memory is a little hazy, says that he believes Bessie "passed" while on the way to the Negro hospital here. He said definitely that the woman was not taken to a white hospital, and wasn't transferred to any other hospital outside of Clarksdale.*

And so, Bessie Smith's blues comeback came to a crashing end while on tour in Mississippi. The rumors of a death fueled by racism proved much more complicated than originally reported, although an atmosphere of segregation clearly played its part in the perfect storm that killed her. Although she wasn't "turned away" from white hospitals, segregation ensured that she would only be taken to a black one—a hospital surely less advanced and capable in 1930s Mississippi.

The "Negro hospital" where Bessie Smith died? G.T. Thomas Afro-American Hospital on Sunflower Avenue in Clarksdale. Today, it is home to the Riverside Hotel.

When I first visited Clarksdale in the 1990s, the Riverside Hotel was situated between two dilapidated juke joints: Rivermount Lounge (911 Sunflower Avenue) and Red's Lounge (395 Sunflower Avenue). The Rivermount partially collapsed in the early 2000s and was bulldozed away. Red's still stands, of course, still offering the blues.

Where Bessie Smith Died, Ike Turner Lived

How much history can a building hold? To get an idea, visit 615 Sunflower Avenue in Clarksdale, Mississippi. That's the address of the Riverside Hotel. If the walls could talk, they'd probably say some of the same things that the hotel's second-generation proprietor, Frank "Rat" Ratliff (1943–2013), told me in 2004.

Ratliff lived in Clarksdale all of his seventy-two years. His mother, Mrs. Z.L. Hill, turned an old African American hospital into a hotel called the Riverside in 1944. Today, it is a long building with multiple rooms, but when she bought it, the main structure only stretched as far as what are now the first two hotel rooms. Ratliff told me that she personally sketched out the expansion plans when she bought the former hospital and hired someone to build the add-on.

After Hill passed away in 1997, Ratliff took over the business full time. He was famous for taking good care of the building, his guests and the location's connection to Mississippi blues history.

One day, he called me at my Cat Head store. He was excited to show me the new flooring he was putting down in part of the hotel. I dropped by

The man himself, Frank "Rat" Ratliff, proprietor of the Riverside Hotel. He always told his guests, "You're home now." *Lou Bopp.*

after work and was (for a moment, anyway) horrified to see the plastic, fake wood planking he was applying to the historic old floor. Then it occurred to me that Frank Ratliff was as much a part of the building's history as his mother was (or Bessie Smith, for that matter), so his new flooring could be grandfathered in, so to speak. In its own way, it was "authentic."

Segregation Meant Business

Ironically, the pre–civil rights segregation of southern blacks and whites meant that, in a sense, there were more business opportunities for African Americans. After all, in many cases, two sets of like businesses were needed within such a community. As author Robert E. Weems Jr. noted in *Desegregating the Dollar: African American Consumerism in the Twentieth Century*, "White-owned businesses, rather than unfettered black consumers, were the primary beneficiaries of the Civil Rights Act of 1964." In other words, as businesses—including hotels—became open to all, many African American consumers took advantage of the wider offering and what was often perceived as a "better" formerly white-only option.

Until the late 1960s, though, segregation still ruled in Mississippi. Traveling African American musicians often relied on both word of mouth and printed guides such as *The Negro Motorist Green Book* (published 1936–66) to find hotels and other accommodations where they could legally spend the night during segregation. The Riverside Hotel first appears in what was often simply called "The Green Book" in 1956, and it is the only African American hotel listed for Clarksdale through the 1963–64 edition, according to copies archived in the New York Public Library Digital Collections.

"This was the only black hotel here in the '40s and the '50s. You didn't have no choice. All those black singers didn't have nowhere else to stay back then," said Ratliff. "They would get a room. Get dressed. Then go and perform and come back. They would eat in here," he noted, pointing to a cozy room just off the hotel lobby. "Mother had the café in here. Mother was a heck of a cook. I learned how to cook from her. If my wife come home with some Jiffy [instant baking mix], I'd throw that stuff away. No Jiffy come in my house!"

According to Ratliff, the Riverside Hotel guest register read like a blues who's who. Among the hundreds of musicians, people like Sonny Boy

Williamson II, John Lee Hooker, Pop Staples, Sam Cooke, the Original Blind Boys, Peck Curtis and many others stayed here through the years. But Mrs. Hill's love of the blues goes back even further than that.

"My mother was a fan of Bessie Smith. She was a blues fan," said Ratliff. "Any time Bessie came to town within a hundred-mile radius, my mother would go to her shows." Because of this fandom and the building's hospital history, it is no wonder that Ratliff's daughter, Zee—the hotel's current, third-generation owner—still preserves the first room off the hotel's reception area, referred to as the "Bessie Smith Room." It is said to be the location of the hospital's operating room.

When talking about such ancient history, Ratliff often reminded visitors that he wasn't born yet when Smith's fateful accident occurred, so he could only repeat things he'd heard from his mother. But he was quick to talk about another musical giant whom he did remember fondly.

"Ike Turner came here around '50," according to Ratliff. "He was about seventeen years old. He was living here with some of his band members. Ike moved over here [from his family's house just across the Sunflower River] because he got too grown and was getting into this band thing. Eugene Fox lived right here on the corner. Jackie Brenston lived in the Brickyard across town."

Birthplace of Rock-and-Roll?

"My mother, her word was just like gold. When they needed instruments for the band, she'd tell them to 'go pick them out and tell Mr. LaVene to call me,'" Ratliff said. LaVene Music Center was a source of both musical instruments and recorded music for many up-and-coming blues players of the time. It was located near the corner of Martin Luther King and Sunflower Avenue where Red's juke joint currently stands open for business. Hill used her store credit to assist Turner with securing instruments. (As an aside, octogenarian bluesman "Big" George Brock once told me he used to buy his harmonicas at LaVene's back in the day as well.)

At the Riverside, "they practiced and rehearsed in the basement. The 'Rocket 88' demo was cut down there. The demo was cut before they went to Memphis and recorded," said Ratliff of Ike and his Kings of Rhythm.

"Rocket 88" with Jackie Brenston on lead vocals—and credited to "Jackie Brenston and his Delta Cats"—is often cited by music historians as the first rock-and-roll song. Is it true, or was it one by Bill Haley, Elvis Presley or Chuck Berry? It doesn't really matter. The point is that it was a pivotal record in the evolution of blues and rock-and-roll. The demo has been lost to time, but based on this information, one could make a case for Clarksdale being the real "Birthplace of Rock-and-Roll" instead of Memphis.

After that legendary trip to Sam Phillips's recording studio in Memphis, Ratliff reported that "they were all excited. I was small. About ten, eleven or twelve during that time. I remember when 'Rocket 88' was a hit because Mother [who was also a seamstress] did the neckties, dresses and things for the band. They would go down to Indianola and different places and play, but this is where they stayed."

Another blues legend who called the Riverside Hotel his home was slide guitar player Robert Lee McCollum, aka Robert Nighthawk, a popular recording artist, local radio star and father to blues drummer Sam Carr. "Robert Nighthawk lived here about four or five years in the '50s," according to Ratliff. When Nighthawk left to go north with his band, Ratliff remembered, "He had to leave a suitcase because he didn't have room enough to put all of the instruments and musicians in the car. So he left his suitcase here with me. I still have the suitcase. He came back looking for it, but Mother had put it in storage. I found it later next

Down the street from the Riverside is Red's juke—once home to LaVene's Music Center, where Ike Turner and others shopped. *Lou Bopp.*

door underneath the house. There was clothes in there, but they had gotten old. I just threw the clothes away. I wish I hadn't now. You want to know the truth? A lot of stuff we didn't put value on."

Ratliff also remembered Alec Rice Miller, aka Sonny Boy Williamson II, saying that he was both interesting and funny. "He carried on with a lot of foolishness. All the King Biscuit boys stayed here. They couldn't go back to Helena if they played in Clarksdale at night. They had to stay here and then catch the ferry back across the river the next day to the twelve o'clock radio show in Helena, Arkansas," he recalled. "In the '50s, everybody listened to *King Biscuit Time* at twelve o'clock. That's when the men would come home, turn their radio on and have their lunches."

As a longtime resident at the epicenter of the Mississippi Delta, Ratliff was also able to paint a vivid picture of the other African American people and places that supported 1940s and '50s blues culture. "You had the old Roxy Theater [beside the site of the recently renovated New Roxy Theater on Issaquena Avenue, downtown]. It was the biggest. Different musicians would come in to play," he said. "They had two shows. They had an early show where parents could bring their kids with blues and comedy, like a fellow dressed up with paint all over his face. Then they had a late show for adults only. We had a twelve o'clock curfew during that time. This town here, at twelve o'clock, baby, you had to be off the streets. If you didn't have a job, you'd go to jail…if you were black. That's how strict it was," he stressed, looking and sounding very serious.

JUKE JOINTS AND GAMBLING HOUSES

Ratliff also recalled some of the personalities surrounding the blues world of the time. "Hardface was a big-time gambler in Tunica," remembered Ratliff. "Hardface was a professional. He played poker, dice and all that. He had a juke house in Tunica. They juked in the front and gambled in the back. A lot of people from here used to go there. There was also a big club in Winstonville [called the Harlem Inn]. That's where all the stars used to go—Little Milton, Ike Turner and them."

Since blues was the pop music of that generation, juke joints and clubs were more common to the Delta landscape then. "How many clubs were there in this town? About forty in the '40s and '50s," he boasted with a chuckle. "Around here you had so many musicians back then. You'd go to this place tonight to hear a band. Tomorrow night you go to another place and hear a band. That's the way it was."

Ratliff still recalled the names of several local jukes—The Green Spot, Day & Night Club, Big House, Leroy's Place—plus many other jukes with names lost to history. Most, he said, were situated between Issaquena and Yazoo Avenue on the African American side of the tracks. Many doubled as cafés and at least one as a rooming house. "Big House was on Fourth Street. It had a blues club in it, and the lady rented rooms on the top floor," he said.

Before Ratliff was born, Clarksdale was even more of a blues town. "In the '30s, this town used to be wide open. This is where all the juke joints were," he noted.

By the time Ratliff was growing up, regional blues bands were more common than the traveling street performers of the Robert Johnson era. "No, they didn't never play on the streets. You had to go to New Orleans to see musicians play on the street. The only somebody you ever saw play on the street was under the viaduct over there on Issaquena. There was a blind man who had a cup and a nickel, and he was shaking it. If you walk up and reach for it, suddenly he wasn't deaf, blind or nothing!" he said with a hearty laugh. "Everybody had a hustle. If you didn't have a hustle, you not going to make it," he explained, returning to his serious look.

Hustling to Survive in the Delta

While Ratliff's mother was certainly not a hustler, she was, in his words, "a very independent lady." "My mother only had one [outside] job in her life," according to Ratliff. "She worked half a day." His mother cooked and cleaned at this employer's home just a single day, he said, "until the white lady said to clean up behind the cat." That sent Mrs. Hill on her way. Besides the hotel, his mother eventually owned a flower shop and a professional seamstress business. "She tied me out on Fourth Street on a rope. People used to pass by there: 'Miss Hill you ought to be ashamed of yourself to have that boy tied out there.' Mother never stopped a beat because she had to pedal that sewing machine." Later, Hill's was one of the few African American households to have both a car and a TV in this small, segregated Delta town. "She was a business-wise person. That's why I'm a business-wise person," he explained.

Like his mother, Ratliff was never afraid of hard work, but he wanted to do it on his own terms. "When people was going to the fields to chop cotton

For years, Riverside Hotel owner "Rat" would send his guests to Red's Lounge and show up to check on them late at night. *Lou Bopp.*

in summertime, I didn't chop cotton. I went out and caught roaches at night and sold them for a penny apiece for fishing. I made fifteen or twenty dollars a day, and you don't get but two dollars a day chopping cotton for eight hours, ten hours."

Until his passing, Ratliff spent most of his days hosting visitors from all over the United States and the world. The Netherlands, France, England, Italy, Germany, Australia, Japan—you name the country, and Ratliff was there to greet them. "This is a hotel, they say. But many call it a home away from home. I give them the keys. They go, and they come. And if they want to come in here and sit down and play music, they're welcome," Ratliff told me with a smile. One such visitor was a guitar-playing Japanese gentleman who went by the name Gypsy. He left his guitar at the Riverside during his first visit in 2002 and has returned for years to soak up the history and hospitality—and play a few tunes. Other musicians, like James "T-Model" Ford of Greenville, were known to drop by for a tune as well. Another notable guest? The late John F. Kennedy Jr., who spent a weekend at the Riverside Hotel in 1991.

More history and mission than job, Ratliff maintained, "I'm here to stay in this business. I was born and brought up in this thing. And I know it. My mother has written a book. I just need to finish it."

In 2013, Frank "Rat" Ratliff was visiting with guests—perhaps reciting from his mother's "book"—when he suffered a heart attack. Today, his only daughter, Zee, keeps the lights on as she writes the next chapter in the history of the juke joint hotel.

RED'S LOUNGE...AND ATTITUDE

As I mentioned earlier, I get music fans and meandering tourists from around the globe at Cat Head every day. Upon their arrival in "Bluestown, USA," they come seeking recommendations for what to see and hear. Typically, I hand them one of my printed *Sounds Around Town* flyers and perhaps an official tourism map of town. Then I tell them about Clarksdale's museums, Mississippi Blues Trail markers, Walk of Fame markers, guitar store, harmonica shop, art galleries and more before launching into my musical recommendations for the night.

I tell you this because occasionally I get a (often older) couple that is seeking entertainment advice for the evening but perhaps not as attuned to blues culture as some. As I run through the "live" music options, I tell them that they should go to as many places as possible, but no matter where else they go, the one essential stop is Red's Lounge—the real juke joint.

Usually, if I recommend it on a given night, folks will go there. And 9.9 times out of 10, they will love it. But occasionally, that less savvy hypothetical couple will drive up to the front of Red's—which, to be fair, barely resembles the front of anything—look at each other and put a foot on the gas.

The next morning, they might even drop by my store again only to say they just couldn't do it. They couldn't cross the threshold of the old, crumbling juke joint to enter the dimly lit music room. My usual response? "Dammit, I was inside, and it was awesome!"

Some may say you can't judge a book by its cover. Maybe. But what if that cover is as it was and always should be? After all, owner Red Paden

Late-night interior shot of Red's juke joint in Clarksdale during production of *We Juke Up in Here! Lou Bopp.*

The self-proclaimed "King of the Juke Joint Runners" himself, Red Paden, keeps an eye out through dark shades. *Lou Bopp.*

once told TV personality Ty Pennington that folks come to him for a "walk on the wild side."

On the Juke Joint Side of the Tracks

Despite trends in disco, rock and hip-hop, despite downtrends in the economy, despite competition from corporate casinos, despite major building repairs and despite the passing of many of Red's friends, musicians and customers, Big Red soldiers on. He fights the good fight—the blues fight—"backed by the river and fronted by the grave."

That quote is a favorite of Red's. It provides both the geography of his juke (which is, indeed, backed by the Sunflower River and fronted by Grange Cemetery) and a veiled threat to potential troublemakers who he sometimes (jokingly) threatens to add his "undertaker's list."

When folks ask why he doesn't renovate his place to compete with clean, contemporary, corporate establishments, he simply says, "It is what it is." Or, as he explained in the film *We Juke Up in Here!*, "I'm the only blues man in this town." Meaning that blues is what he does. He is the pro here, not to be questioned. He knows why people walk through his door.

Some might say he's simply stubborn, but for me, since I came from a professional brand-building, marketing background, what appears to be stubbornness on the surface is actually on par with what Apple and Nike do out in the so-called real world. This is Branding 101. Create a unique or unusual product, find a customer for that product and keep a consistent message (look, feel, attitude) in the face of all competition. Differentiate, don't duplicate. Don't water down your brand or try to be something that you are not. Stay true to self. Stay authentic.

Of course, that doesn't mean things haven't evolved through the years. When I finally moved to Clarksdale in 2002 after a half dozen years of visiting, the size of Red's audience would range wildly from a couple people to a packed house. But at that time, it consisted almost entirely of middle aged and up African Americans. It was common for Red to step out from behind the bar back then and announce, "It's white night!" with a chuckle, whenever the scale tipped to be more white than black faces on the bar stools.

While Red has done his best to ignore the African American community's generational shifts from blues music to R&B, from soul to hip-hop, his customer has not. Many—maybe most—of his old-school friends and customers from his venue's glory days have simply died or become too old to go out at night. Others now spend their entertainment dollars up at the casinos in Tunica, Mississippi. And a few have turned away from the juke and back to church. After all, blues is still the "Devil's Music" in land of the "Crossroads."

And the young folks? Unfortunately (for blues, anyway), most want today's pop music and preferably from a deejay, not a "live" band.

Old Brand for a New Customer

Just as Red has refused to update his ancient building, he has also refused to drastically update his music. He continues to offer as traditional of blues acts (mostly African American) as he can find, and in recent years, he has built up his weekly music nights to include Wednesday, Thursday, Friday, Saturday and Sunday. During festivals, he often runs for one or even two weeks straight. And speaking of festivals, in 2018, he held his first-ever Red's Old-Timers Blues Festival just a block from his business; it was a festival only open to blues musicians who were sixty years old and up; his oldest was ninety-one-year-old "Cadillac" John Nolden.

What does this have to do with Red's brand? To paraphrase brand-man Joseph Pine, what makes our tourists happy is spending time and money satisfying the desire for authenticity. Red continues to provide that authenticity—societal trends be damned.

Speaking of the owner, Red is as much the star of the show as his bands or venue at this point. He is a legend in blues circles. As he is a past recipient of the Sunflower River Blues Association's Early Wright Award and the Blues Foundation's Keeping the Blues Alive Award, tourists, photographers, filmmakers and others often seek out the man himself for selfies and interviews. And his notoriety nearly led to something even bigger.

Red really is one of the last in his generation to be actively running a "live" blues juke joint—and the world has taken notice.

Big Red Almost Goes "Hollywood"

In February 2014, a producer named Josh Murphy called me out of the blue from North Hollywood, California. He worked for a company that created those horrible reality shows that took over TV in the first decade and a half of the new millennium.

He was a music fan (and actually a very cool guy) and searching for something different than the *Survivor* and *Atlanta Housewives* types of shows—something perhaps closer to *Pawn Shop* but with good music and a southern attitude. He wanted to pitch a reality show based in a Mississippi juke joint. Since there were so few left, and even fewer with something approaching a "staff," Red's seemed like the natural choice.

Now, for the record, I was kind of against this idea. I was afraid that Hollywood might trump authenticity, that publicity and fame might ruin the real deal. Still, when I hung up from Murphy, I called Red. He saw green and asked me to pursue it for him. I e-mailed Josh, and he asked for a potential "cast of characters." The edited version that follows gives you an idea of what I sent him and why a juke joint ain't just another blues club.

Partial Cast of Characters

RED (not his real first name, but don't ask): The late sixties ringleader runs his forty-year-old juke joint (his third) as a quasi-legal house party at his home away from home—since he doesn't want you at his actual house. He's known for enigmatic sayings like "I'm backed by the river and fronted by the grave," "The game's for life" and "I kill for fun!" Famous musicians and movie stars from around the globe have graced his doorway, and TV shows and music videos have been filmed at his haunt. Red is the only local club owner who throws blues birthday parties for his regular, older blues performers and customers. He also includes me in this, though two years out of the past three, the banners and/or cakes have misspelled my first and/or last names. Classic.

DR. DINGO (aka the Australian Dog): Just to be clear, Dingo was not a real doctor. "Dr." is a prefix assigned to several of the juke joint deejays in the region, but I must say, Dr. Dingo was definitely a prescription

"We can have a good time in here. But you ain't fixing to mess with my money," according to juke owner Red Paden. *Lou Bopp.*

A longtime Red's regular lights up in front of her evening's beverage selection as the blues music plays on. *Lou Bopp.*

for a good time. Around Red's age, Dingo thought he worked at the classic juke. He'd thought this for years. He helped Red take out the trash, MCed between band sets, spun CDs when the bands go on break, acted as doorman and more. Still, he was not only unpaid for his efforts, but he was also generally and consistently yelled at by Red. It was all in good fun—I think. He was so beloved by tourists that they traveled from out of town for his birthday party each year and sent him photos and cards via my Cat Head store.

MISS MAE: A longtime Red's customer through all three of his juke joints, and around the same age, Miss Mae has her own table at Red's for her and her equally tough, blues-loving older lady friends who still occasionally accompany her. Her main sidekick is the quick-to-smile, rare-to-speak Miss Eura. As a duo, they sit behind their table of multiple eighteen-ounce beer bottles and the occasional Crown Royal bottle. While she will sometimes get up to cut a rug on the dance floor, generally Miss Mae spends most of her time at her table laughing with Eura, yelling at Red and shouting opinions at the band. Buy her a drink and give her a hug and she's a friend for life. (As a side note, I was in Norway with some bluesmen for a festival a few years back. As our van slowly rolled into downtown Notodden, I glanced to my right only to see an enormous photo enlargement filling a shop window. It was a black-and-white shot of Miss Mae, holding down her table at Red's. She'd gone international! I told her about it upon my return. She stared at me for a long second and then turned back toward the band and took a swig of beer, unimpressed.)

COBURN: In his late forties, maybe, Coburn races motorcycles, works for the local power company as a lineman and occasionally operates as the comedian bartender at Red's. He can recite old Red Foxx monologues verbatim and sing the *B.J. and the Bear* TV show theme song with glee. He invited me to come to one of his home yard parties with Red one time. We sat outside his place drinking heavily and talking trash for hours. The only other white guy at the yard party kept passing out and falling straight back off his picnic table seat. He'd wake up upon impact. The guys would laugh and pick him back up, and he'd drink some more and then fall straight back again. Another time, back at the juke, Coburn and Red cracked themselves up telling me about some of the blues characters from the old days. One was a strongman called "Rockin' Red" who they swore used to hug trees, shake them from side to side to loosen the roots and pull them straight out of the ground for fun. Another was a long-armed muscleman called "Monkey Man" who got picked up by the cops one night out front of Red's. After a fight that involved the hard-drinking Monkey Man slamming the officers up against the front of Red's with such force that it was heard inside, law enforcement finally got cuffs on him—which, according to my storytellers, he broke out of inside the squad car. They finally got him into a cell at the city jail only to walk halfway down the hallway turn and see that Monkey Man was right behind them, having already broken out. True or not, we all laughed at the telling.

BIG CHARLES: This sixty-something character—with a personality as big as his physical displacement—has no patience for nonsense or deadbeats, but he does have the patience to bake homemade cakes for friends. In fact, locally, he's a bit famous for his strawberry cake. Besides helping Red out behind the bar serving beers and emptying big buckets of empties, Charles has a day job as a shade tree mechanic. Like most mechanics I know in town, he drives a vehicle that you hear way before you see it—presumably a "good deal" that was saved from the junkyard. Whenever Charles is at Red's, there is the possibility of some philosophizing at the bar. He is a hilarious, thoughtful man. One night, he kept trying to tell me something, but I couldn't understand a single word. Later, he explained that he was just showing me his skill as a ventriloquist. Once or twice a year, he'll challenge Red's champion dancer (Ellis, to follow) to a bit of a dance-off in front of the band. Now, I'm not going to say he can "outdance" Ellis, but to his credit, to see a man of his considerable girth glide around the old dance floor is quite a sight to behold.

ELLIS: The younger brother of a local blues star, Ellis is a bit of a "ladies' man"—or perhaps used to be. Now, he is the happily married, jheri-curled, sharp-dressed, smiling face in a cowboy hat who asks all the fine-looking tourists and local ladies to dance. As a boyfriend or husband in the audience, if you didn't know better, you'd think he was trying to steal your lovely lady—and frankly, on a good night, he probably could. But actually he's just enjoying himself and adding to this classic juke joint floorshow. He comes from a day when all the ladies were local and every night out was a dance party. He and Big Charles sometimes get into a friendly dance

Juke joint legend Red Paden jokes with filmmakers after doing a little carpentry work on his aging juke joint exterior. *Lou Bopp.*

competition, but for Ellis, there really isn't any competition. (Since I can't dance and can prove it, Ellis often jokes about me "taking over for him" when he "goes on break.")

So, Did the TV Show Get Made?

No. But, the producer had me set up a series of Skype video calls with local blues players and characters in an effort to create a "sizzle tape" that would convince his bosses to greenlight the project—or at least the creation of an actual pilot episode to sell to cable TV.

The resulting sizzle tape was ridiculous. If I were a bigwig in Hollywood, I would have choked on my Emmy and flipped the switch on that greenlight posthaste.

I set up taped Skype video calls with several musicians and our town's mayor, but the call that beat them all was the one at Red's. I borrowed a portable Wi-Fi hotspot from a friend and took my Mac laptop down to the dimly lit juke. I'd asked Red to assemble his blues posse, so they were ready to go when I got there. From Hollywood via the world wide web, Josh finally met the characters I'd told him about. One by one, Dr. Dingo, Coburn, Ellis and so on took to the video call.

When Dingo was on the call, his buddies all kept chiming in to give him a hard time. As Red would say, "That was just proper procedure!"

Coburn refused to sing the theme to early 1980s TV classic *B.J. and the Bear*, feigning ignorance once put on the spot. But he did agree to tell a joke. Unfortunately, it happened to be perhaps the most "adult" joke I have ever personally heard. In fact, I cannot even approach the subject matter here if I hope to get this book published. Let it suffice to say that a local friend of mine walked through Red's door with his teenage daughter just as the punchline was being delivered, only to turn right around and hurry his daughter back out the door. (I was so embarrassed. He'd brought his daughter to see a young, local blues prodigy Christone "Kingfish" Ingram perform that night. Oh well.)

Ellis played his part as the ladies' man in his on-screen interview, saying, "I'm the party man around Red's. I got to get down. I got to kick a leg, baby. If the music is right? I got to get up. I got to party!" He was coming across super smooth and debonair when—and I swear this is true—out of the blue his wife bursts through the door at Red's with a red rose in hand to wish her husband "happy anniversary," unaware he was on a video call with Hollywood. The Red's posse burst out laughing, and Ellis was, for once, totally speechless.

Red was his normal juke joint outlaw, blues-gangster self. He rolled through his classic sayings—some original, some poached from movies—and played up the rough-and-tumble nature of the old juke joint days. He came off as what he is: a rock star in the blues idiom.

Big Charles insisted on going last, so (in his words) he could "correct everyone else's bull----." He was charming and funny, if a bit inebriated. At one point, he started talking about how all of this blues came from sweating it out in the cotton fields of the Mississippi Delta. After a hard week of work, you simply had to let off the pressure at a juke like Red's. Then he let it slip that he himself had never actually chopped cotton, and the posse again erupted with laughter.

Sure, the TV show never got made, but the night of the sizzle tape recording was a fascinating one. It really showcased juke joint culture and the camaraderie of this particular crew of longtime blues friends. To quote Charles that night, "This is a family. This whole club is a family." And oh, what a family. From the Skype call:

> *Charles: "What makes a blues club an authentic old blues club is when you walk in the door, that blues club's just like a poor man's house. S---, he ain't got no money to go out there and buy no damn matching chairs. When you walk in there, shoot, there ain't no matching tables, ain't no matching chairs. He just bought what he could get!"*
>
> *Coburn: "Woo! The place gets so crowded that people can't get to the bar. They're passing money, and I'm passing beers through the crowd. Most of the time the people run out of money before I run out of funny."*
>
> *Red: "I'm grouchy. It's my way, or it's no damn way!"*
>
> *Dingo: "These guys always bustin' my chops."*
>
> *Charles: "You got to have somebody to pick on."*
>
> *Red: "Dr. Dingo is scandalous. You have to watch him at all times!"*

Sadly, the good doctor, Dingo, passed away in 2017. And while the TV show idea also passed away, fortunately Red's lives on to this day—every night, every bit a reality show.

IF THE WALLS COULD TALK, PART II

Self-described "Mississippi boogie" musician Jimbo Mathus of Corinth, Mississippi, often talks about "antique musics," of which blues is certainly one. It reaches back through generations of mostly African American southerners, especially those from the Magnolia State. In Part II of my blues interview excerpts, we'll hear from a range of (mostly) "antique" characters. Regardless of the generation, many of the stories and observations strike a fascinatingly similar chord.

JOHN HORTON (GREENVILLE, MISSISSIPPI)

There was a club, man. We started out playing for—okay this was big money for us—twenty dollars for the band [laughs]. Me and my guys, we knew about four or five songs. Five dollars a piece. Man, we were ready. And that little old place, it could take but ten or fifteen people, and you couldn't move in there. Boy, they'd be waiting on us on Saturday night, though. I'm telling you. But something happened there. This is what stopped me from drinking. This didn't happen but once in life. I was so nervous. I went to the bar, got me a half pint of gin and eased outside. Boy, I had the shakes. I tore that son up. I came back in there. I played like one song and said, "Will y'all excuse me a minute?" I don't even know what made me walk out. So, I went out of the place. The next thing I knew, I woke up and was way out in the field—way across the field, man. I was lost. I was looking around. I said, "Man, where am I at?" And I could see a post light about a mile across there. My mind kind of cleared up a little bit, I said, "I'm supposed to be doing a show" [laughs]. So, when I made it back to the club, they had put my stuff back in my van. I had my van and car there. It didn't end there. I was like in the front room, and boy, it was spinning. It finally slowed down, and I peeped out the door and realized my car was out there and the van. I said, "Well, I'm going to get that car." They didn't want me to drive. So, I got in the car and was going home, and I stopped for some reason or another, and when I woke up, it was the next day, and I was lost again. The car was out of gas. The battery was down. I had done fallen asleep. It took me a minute to figure it out. I said, "Oh, man." I was about five miles from my house. I was nineteen or twenty. I haven't been drunk since.

JAMES "SUPER CHIKAN" JOHNSON (CLARKSDALE, MISSISSIPPI)

At Junior Kimbrough's juke joint they brought me that moonshine. It looked like water. I was sipping out of that stuff. It went down so smooth. When it was time to go, I stepped outside, and I went blind. I couldn't even find my car. Somebody was hollering, "Hey man, where you going? Here's your car over hear" [laughs]. Josh "Razorblade" Stewart drove me home.

MARTIN "BIG BOY" GRANT (SENATOBIA, MISSISSIPPI)

They also say that the Rolling Stones stopped in Junior's joint once. You'd see people from Holland and Italy and all over the world in there. They'd heard about Junior's, and they flocked to it. Kind of like here in Clarksdale. The "Crossroads" draws everybody here. Mostly, folks drank Budweiser or Bud Light, but they also had moonshine. They had a guy selling it out of his trunk. They couldn't sell it in the building, but *you could get it out of his trunk. So, everybody'd have moonshine. At one time, he had "chartered" moonshine where he'd filtered it through some coal, and that charcoal flavored it a little bit and gave it a little bit of that whiskey color. And it went down a little smoother. But if you didn't drink all your drink that night when you were partying and you looked at it the next morning, sometimes you'd have black s--- floating in it, so it ain't real good!* [Laughs.]

L.C. ULMER (ELLISVILLE, MISSISSIPPI)

Blues was all there was. It started in the cotton fields. Ever since they built a cotton field in the state of Mississippi, the blues started there. The blues started in Mississippi, and you know, they tried to wear it down, but it's coming back strong. Now, I can play all over the guitar. 'Cause I played too many jukes by myself. Didn't need nobody to help me. When I was in Chicago [in the 1960s], *they fired the band and hired me to play the place as a one-man band 'cause I was playing twelve pieces. They fired many a people in Chicago and put me on the stage. I kept my own time with my drum and cymbals. I started playing as a one-man band in 1949.*

DAVID LEE DURHAM (INDIANOLA, MISSISSIPPI)

There was a bunch of little juke joints in the country then, and there was a juke joint in Inverness called the Harlem Club. That's where the Howlin' Wolf played, and B.B. played there, too. Muddy Waters, Elmore James and all them played at that place. When I was little, I used to go there and watch the Howlin' Wolf play. I used to love watching him. I was too young to go in there, so I'd go to the window and stand up on a five-gallon bucket and look through the window. One time, Howlin' Wolf was playing at the Harlem Club, and they got to fighting in there. And they ran out the back door and ran over me! [Laughs.] *I won't never forget that! That place would be jammed pack. It was a place about the size of Club Ebony. Maybe a little bigger. I never seen Elmore James play there, but they said he played there. I seen the Muddy Waters play there. He put on a good show, too, but my favorite was the Howlin' Wolf. I looked in the window and seen him.*

JIMMY "DUCK" HOLMES (BENTONIA, MISSISSIPPI)

I seen Howlin' Wolf once in Yazoo City years ago. A place called Silver Slipper. When he got up on that stage—shoot! Look, he lost it! He done lost it. When he got up and got that harmonica, he took the roof off the building. He had that blues in him. Yes, sir. In those days, when it came to country blues, hardcore blues, no two people played alike. I'll tell you why: blues is like your relationship with Christ. It's personal. What drives me to sing the blues don't drive you. My emotions—things I talk about in a song, things that drive me to sing—ain't the same things that drive you. It can't be the same.

Blue Front Café in Bentonia, Mississippi, doesn't offer regular shows, but when it does feature music, the joint is rocking. *Lou Bopp.*

"BIG" GEORGE BROCK (MISSISSIPPI/MISSOURI)

When I left Clarksdale, we was playing over in Charleston, Mississippi. Me, Lee Kizart and a guy called Hound Dog. We were playing. The police walked in and told us we had fifteen minutes to get this s--- out of here, and we left town. I didn't go back over to Charleston no more. And I came to Walls, Mississippi, and then I run into Howlin' Wolf in the back of a theater on Monday nights, so I started playing with him.

DAVID "HONEYBOY" EDWARDS (MISSISSIPPI/CHICAGO)

Charley Patton died in '34. When Charley was performing in the Delta at the time, you know he was just all over. He played in Rosedale, Drew, Ruleville, Cleveland, Merigold, Leland. He was just in the middle. Everybody knowed him. And at that time, a lot of peoples in the country would have country dances, and there was a lot of people in the country making white whiskey. That's how they made their living, off making whiskey. We played then in mostly private houses. They had a couple clubs around there in Clarksdale. A lot of people gambled then. Clarksdale used to be open. They had dives in Clarksdale in the black neighborhood. You paid the shakedown. Paid the police shakedown. Most of the money would come out of the country from those farmers. There was gambling all through the plantations.

BUD SPIRES (BENTONIA, MISSISSIPPI)

After a while, I got up blowing around good for myself, by myself, and I run up on Jack Owens. He was picking guitar. I said, "Jack?" "What you want, boy?" "You mind me trying to blow a little?" "No, boy, get your harp and try to blow with me. We might start up something." Jack used to farm. He farmed up until he quit when he was playing the blues. Now, he wasn't playing the blues for a living. He sell his own corn whiskey when he started running his juke joint at his house. His wife, Mable, she'd fry fish and cook them chitlins. She had a big old cooker that would hold two five-pound buckets. She ain't clean none of them and take and dump them over in that cooker. And she'd cut 'em up. And everybody crazy about 'em, too. They'd be tender done. They wasn't nasty or nothing.

"Dr. Feelgood" Potts (Mississippi/Memphis)

I used to sit in with the bands that came to Greenwood. Back then, it wasn't a thing that you had to be a certain age to go into these juke joints. There wasn't nobody who was going to stop you from going in there. Sometimes there would be house parties where they would be gambling and drinking their homemade liquor and stuff. 'Course I didn't do no drinking or gambling or nothing. I was just a little kid, and I'd just wander off into there. If my parents had known I was in there, they would have whipped me all the way home [laughs]. *I would go, like, "Can I sing a song with y'all?" Sometimes it would take me all night to get up the courage to go ask the musicians. Then I'd break out on a Jimmy Reed or a John Lee Hooker song, and they would be accompanying me.*

Cedell Davis (Arkansas/Mississippi)

I was born in Helena, Arkansas, June 9, 1927. My stepfather worked in West Helena. But I didn't hardly live with him and my mother. I lived with a cousin of mine in Mississippi. Right outside of Tunica—what they call Clayton. The juke joints have always been around Tunica, but when I was playing there, they didn't have casinos. Now, they have 16. There was plenty of gambling going on in the juke joints, though.

Bill Abel (Duncan, Mississippi)

One time I was playing with my eyes closed at Johnson's Grocery with David Lee Durham in Shaw, Mississippi. And a voice goes, "This is the police. Put your hands up." So, I opened my eyes, and there was a policeman with a gun pointed at everybody. Earlier that day, the police chief and the owner of the juke joint got into an argument. So he got mad at him and went to arrest him for having gambling in the back which he'd been having for twenty or thirty years. I've seen people pull guns, but I've never seen anybody shot or stabbed or nothing. Usually, everybody's real nice. The older crowds are into blues, and the younger crowd usually leaves when we start playing. So, it's safe that way.

Juke joints and house parties have always been community meeting places for blues lovers.
Lou Bopp.

Mark "Mule Man" Massey (Senatobia, Mississippi)

I was born in Clarksdale, Mississippi, in 1969. They call me the "Mule Man" 'cause I sell and trade horses, mules, cattle, chicken. But mostly, I'm in love with my mules. The first couple years of my life, my dad had a job here in Clarksdale, and then he was on the road a lot with Gulf Finance Company. He had a lot of the loans with the local juke joint guys here in Clarksdale. The first music that I can probably remember would have been old country, and my dad was a huge blues guy who listened to a lot of your Howlin' Wolf, Muddy Waters and Lightnin' Hopkins. When my dad was riding the back roads and drinking beer, I would be in the back of the truck, and we would stop at these juke joints. I remember getting out of the truck, and he would force me into watching these blues guys play—which now I see there was a reason behind it all.

"Blind Mississippi" Morris Cummings (Mississippi/Memphis)

At that time, Fourth Street in Clarksdale was a jumping spot. And Yazoo was jumping. My little half-brother's grandmother owned one of the first black taverns in that town—a juke joint called the Do Drop Inn. Her name was Mattie Mae Epps. My mom had a baby by Epps's son. She had it going on—even a dancing chicken! The chicken danced, man [laughs]. When she'd tell him to dance, he'd get out there and cut a rug. Yeah. She'd put her little jukebox on, and that rooster would cut a shine. He was one of the top acts, I guess, around that town. He couldn't sing or play, but he sure could dance. He also drank beer.

David "Honeyboy" Edwards

Clarksdale used to be a hell of a town, Clarksdale. And a lot of musicians lived around Clarksdale. Pinetop Perkins drove a tractor out there at Hopson [Plantation]. He was staying out there back in '37, '38. We had a little juke on Hopson, but mostly Pinetop drove a tractor and played out at house parties around Lambert and Tutwiler. We played all around there, out to Jonestown and Lula up there at Jones Plantation. Muddy Waters used to stay in a little old house and drive a tractor there at Stovall [Plantation], not too far from Clarksdale. I think he had house parties every once and a while and sold white whiskey like that. All them hustled a little bit out there and played on the streets.

Mary Ann "Action" Jackson
(Senatobia, Mississippi)

Back in the day, there were more house parties for blues than clubs—'cause there weren't many clubs out in the country. My hometown, Senatobia, was a dry county, so they'd have to go out and get the booze and stuff and bring it back. And everybody would get together and gather at their houses. Like we do out at R.L. Boyce's now? That's how it was. We'd all get together and have a foot-stompin' good time like that. And it wouldn't be a blues party without fried fish or barbecue or something. There's got to be some food and drinks. You've got to have something to drink. Now, back then, all there was was moonshine and homebrew. My mother used to make the wine and have it up under the cabinet. Homemade stuff. With it being a "dry county" like it was, we knew how to do things. We knew how to make wine out of pears or corn cobs or whatever they used to make it out of. Mmm hmm.

Robert "Wolfman" Belfour
(Red Banks, Mississippi)

When I was a teenager, I used to play at these open houses, you know. They give you a few dollars and all the white whiskey you want to drink, all the fish you want to eat. Places like that, anybody could play. [Nowadays] I like Red's Lounge in Clarksdale. It's kind of a quiet place. It's a nice place, and the people there is nice. Red, I like. You know, I enjoy him. Me and him are kind of old brothers. He's a good guy, yeah. We brothers [laughs]. And I've met some more nice mens and womens since I been coming down there. Everybody treats me nice. I like playing down there. The people say, "You just make people feel good when they hear the music, and there's just something about your music that just do something to peoples. It's like it hypnotize them or something." I say, "Well, I ain't trying to hypnotize them" [laughs]. They just love to hear you. It brings back memories of things in life. Sometimes I'm liable to play for two hours straight before I even stop.

Louis "Gearshifter" Youngblood
(Jackson, Mississippi)

My Uncle Arzo was a hardworking man, as far as I could tell. And on the weekends, on Friday and Saturday nights, he'd play guitar, and they'd cook and sell fish and have a wang dang doodle around the house. When they wasn't at his house, they were at somebody else's house. And that's what he did. Went from house to house. He wasn't too much of a juke joint person. He was mostly around the houses, from one house to the next. Whatever they had was mostly like house sessions. You always cooking something and have something around. I didn't get to follow him around too much, but the little that I did. Shoot, it was like a way of life. That was when I first got familiar with the smell of beer. The taste of whiskey. It was so strong, I said, "Why they like this?" Beer was nasty, and whiskey was strong. Shoot. I try to keep it under control 'cause it will get you in plenty of trouble. They got some stuff now you really don't need to fool with if you want to function. They had plenty of that clear white whiskey. They had like a jar, a jug, and you couldn't take much of that, or things get real cloudy! [Laughs.] Well, I guess I became an alcoholic to a certain point, at one time. I had to go through some things to help me back up off it. It hurts sometimes when something has to happen to you in order for you to think, but that's the best lesson. My mom told me, "Bought sense is the best kind!" [Laughs.]

JAMES "T-MODEL" FORD (GREENVILLE, MISSISSIPPI)

The first time I went on to Nelson Street [in Greenville] *I was sitting on the porch. All them women was around me. They was dancing and drinking that damn corn whiskey. Here come an old man in a pickup. He pulled up in there and got out. He said, "Why don't you quit wasting your time and go on and make you some money?" I said, "Well, I don't know if I'm that good enough to make any money." He said, "You play as good as anyone play a guitar.* [Local bluesman] *Booba Barnes and them can't handle you." He said, "If I can get you to play tonight, will you play?" I said, "Yeah." He went on down to this man's café that was just opening and asked him, "Do you need a guitar player?" He said, "Go get him and bring him down here." By eight o'clock, all the people done left Booba and them down the street and come in and lined the tables up. You couldn't get in that place. I was the boss of Nelson, and I'm still the boss of Nelson. I been the bad man ever since then.*

BUD SPIRES

I was about twelve when I first heard a guy picking a guitar and another picking a piano. It was at a house. Back then, they called them jukes. One was Cornelius Bright and the other was Bud Slater. They gone now. Man, I loved it, 'cause, see, my daddy was a musician. He first started with a harp. That's the way I started, with a harp. I was five years old. Santa Claus brought me the first one. Back that long, they had them high-priced guitars. He said, "No, boy, I'll give you a harp. I ain't going to give you a guitar" [laughs]. *Back then, for a harp, you didn't pay but twenty-five cents. I got one now, it was thirty-five dollars. When I was about nine or ten, my daddy left and went to Chicago and played a while up there. You ain't heard some of them pieces he put out? They called him* [Arthur] *"Big Boy" Spires. That was him.*

"CADILLAC" JOHN NOLDEN (RENOVA, MISSISSIPPI)

Back then, [blues musicians] *played on weekends. They'd come on Friday night or Saturday, like that. In fact, they had these little parties at the house. Little corn whiskey. They'd have a time. Sometimes you go in there, and there wouldn't be but one musician. Nobody helping him at all—just him and his guitar. A little corn whiskey, and folks dancing. A couple of them places could be dangerous. You know what I mean? I didn't go up in those places too much. You can get up in there, and them folks head banging and all that stuff. Sometimes you have to kind of find your way out of there. Things get so rough in there. I didn't like that whiskey-drinking stuff.*

MARY ANN "ACTION" JACKSON

R.L. Boyce's house parties are like "boom, boom, boom" [laughs and starts singing, "Goin' Down South"]. *You done been there before. You know. They have a good time. Every time I go down there, they have a yard full of people, and they're kicking up dust. There was another juke joint out there in Marshall County. It was so nice, but they was hating out there and burned it down. It was a good juke joint. Everybody would come on out there to eat, drink and dance. But somebody burned it down. It was a trailer that they'd built and added on to it—had a beauty shop in the back. It was real nice. It got burned down about six or eight months ago. I don't know how long, but it ain't been too long. I like Clarksdale. Period. I play at Ground Zero Blues Club and Tricia's and Red's. And I've been at Cat Head before. I got tickled. Man, we was having a good time. I live in Memphis now. I've been out there to Wild Bill's but not since Wild Bill died. I really like ole Wild Bill's juke joint.*

Steve "Lightnin'" Malcolm (North Mississippi)

I can't remember the first time I met R.L. Boyce. We probably met at Otha Turner's picnic. R.L. Boyce has got a sound like nobody else has got. He's got that rhythm like Fred McDowell or something. I don't know how to explain it, but nobody else can do it. Even though there are guys thinking they're close. Sometimes I think I'm close. But when I hear him, it's like, "No, you're not even in the ballpark." It don't matter that R.L. don't know that many songs 'cause he can make the most riveting song out of just whatever's happening right around him. His house is just like a juke joint. Every night, the driveway is going to be full of cars. People drinking and playing. At R.L. Burnside's house, it was always fun, too. There was no telling who was going to pull up in his driveway. It might be a tour bus or limousine or just the moonshine man.

R.L. Boyce (Como, Mississippi)

The Otha Turner picnics have been going as long as I know. Ever since I been in the world. The weekend in August, they have one every year. Back in the day, it was different than things is now. 'Cause things back then when I was playing drums, you usually had to put it by the fire and let that head warm up. And boy, you could hear that thing from here to Mars. But now, if it get cooled down, it'll go down. You put it by that fire and let it warm up. [Imitates drum sound.] *"Uh oh, they're playing over there at Otha's." Back then, when I was playing with Otha, man, I used to lay on my back with one stick in my mouth and one in my hand, and heat that bass drum up. But, see, the older you get, you go down that road. See, I got shot back in '85. It's a long story. But my back made it so I couldn't play like I used to. Couldn't nobody beat me playing that bass drum back then.*

Otha is dead and gone. That's one man who used to depend on me. He used to tell me, "We got to leave. Let's go." He couldn't read. But me and him stuck together. The two that could really play that fife was Napolean and Otha. See, Napolean could beat Otha, but Otha always thought he could beat Napolean.

Jimmy "Duck" Holmes

See, when my father and them first got [the Blue Front], *where you see the little window, that was the serving window. You used to walk to the counter and order food that my mother prepared in the back. Also, that wall was full of shelves. Really, it was a mini store, or you could say it was a convenience store. They sold meal, flour, lard, canned goods. That wall was full of stuff. Then, in the back was a pressing room where you press clothes. A lady back there used to bring clothes from the wash and press them.* [Out here, there were] *food tables. A pool table set here. A jukebox set in that corner. There were nine windows. Originally, there wasn't no electric, so my mom used these windows for the sunlight. They put electric in here after my mom and father took it over. Prior to that, there wasn't any electric. You can see* [the windows] *boarded up. I'm the one who had them boarded up. My momma said they used to come out around late Saturday afternoon. They'd come through with their guitars and come and sit out front. It wasn't no scheduled thing. Someone would come through with a guitars or wanted to play harmonica.*

Steve "Lightnin'" Malcolm

Odell Harris is one of my favorite partners who I don't get to see too often. When I met Odell, he was living up there in Nesbit. He just had a little shack out there. The only running water was a little hose out there in the yard. When you pull up in his driveway, you know you're dealing with a maniac. I mean, there's just no question about it. There's tiles and shingles and about fifty automobiles lined up out there in various states.

Tools everywhere. Trash everywhere. He had like a little electric skillet sitting out on the porch, and that's what he cooked from. The first night I was there, we were drinking a lot of moonshine and didn't eat for a while. You know, we got carried away playing music. Later on that night, he was talking about how he was going to cook something. He pulled this damn electric skillet off the porch, dumped out the grease, had a knife that was laying around. He cut up this damn chicken, and I was sitting there thinking, "Man, there ain't no way I'm eating that chicken. I'll just go hungry tonight. He's going to kill somebody." I got to messing around and kept playing guitar. He put them peppers and onions in there. Man, it smelled so good. Finally, I was like, "Hell, give me a piece." That was some of the best chicken. Odell could cook! He's a lot like T-Model Ford—just unstoppable.

SHACK UP INN CO-FOUNDER GUY MALVEZZI (CLARKSDALE, MISSISSIPPI)

In the late 1960s, I was buying beer, shooting pool and playing pinball machines in local jukes where the blues was being played, and like most white kids back then, the British invasion made me aware of the music. Then, starting in the 1980s, I'd see tourists just wandering around looking for anything associated with blues or Delta history.

RED PADEN (CLARKSDALE, MISSISSIPPI)

I enjoy all these tourists. Most of them are just thrilled to be here and hear this blues music that they didn't know still exists. There's nothing like an old-time juke where they come from. I get folks from all over the world. Every weekend is like a big old-school house party at Red's place. Ain't nobody going to change that. And that's for damn sure!

Anthony "Big A" Sherrod
(Clarksdale, Mississippi)

Nowhere but here. This is the only juke joint left. Red's Lounge.

Christone "Kingfish" Ingram
(Clarksdale, Mississippi)

There was a band that used to stay beside me, where I lived here in Clarksdale on Pecan Street. A blues band. I was very young then. I would hear music right directly beside me. One day, I was outside with my guitar, and this singer called "Spiderweb" said, "Hey man, come on in." When I went in, there was Wesley "Junebug" Jefferson, Lee Williams, "Dr. Mike" James. It was just all these guys playing blues in there. They really inspired me. A lot of "characters"! All of them.

Former child prodigy—now a sharp young man—Christone "Kingfish" Ingram is Mississippi's bluesman to watch. *Lou Bopp*.

ROBERT KIMBROUGH SR.
(HOLLY SPRINGS, MISSISSIPPI)

My name is Robert Kimbrough Sr. I was born in Holly Springs, Mississippi, on June 11, 1968. The first thing I remember is the church-going thing. My mom always kept us in church, but with my dad, the blues was there at all times. The blues just sort of took over, and we started having house parties. We stayed out on Hernando Road then, and my dad would have outside parties. The yard would just be covered with people from everywhere. My dad would play, and then you had like R.L. Burnside, my dad's band with Little Joe Ayers and the crew, and there might have been a couple more who played. I was pretty young back then, so I was just doing a lot of dancing [laughs].

JIMMY "DUCK" HOLMES

Strangely enough, when I was a child growing up, black people only partied on Saturday night. You had a few of them partied on Friday. Now, when I was a kid, Saturday was a workday. Just as hard as Monday through Friday. Only difference was that most people would get off around noon on Saturday. Saturday morning was a workday. Sunday was strictly a church day from early Sunday morning 'til nine or ten Sunday night. 'Cause we'd go to Sunday school and worship service. Come home and eat, and go back Sunday evening for prayer service. That was routine in the black community. Sunday was totally sacred. See the same faces on Saturday night, see them Sunday. Does that make them sinful? I don't think so. The only difference between now and then is you had entire families that so together that they set aside Sunday for God. Now, you got maybe one or two family members who go to church on Sunday. In other words, mothers and fathers don't demand their kids to go to church.

Terry "Harmonica" Bean (Pontotoc, Mississippi)

I didn't realize what was happening 'til I met this guy in Greenville. He was a preacher. He would always come when T-Model was playing around there. He would pop up. He told me that I played the harmonica well, you know. I said, "Yeah, I play pretty good." He said, "No, you play real well, but if you don't play it right, it will send you to hell!" That's what he told me. That kind of scared me 'cause I didn't know what it meant. So I told T-Model about it, and I also brought it up to Willie Foster. They didn't know what he meant by it either. Well, one night we was playing in Moorehead, and T-Model was playing the guitar, I was blowing the harmonica, John was on the drums, and this guy was singing for us named Jerry. Jerry was flirting with this woman he liked, and he was singing to her, and a fight broke out. Knives come out. They cut the guy, too. That's when it dawned on me what the preacher was telling me: If you're playing it just for fun, that's all right. But if you see somebody out there you like and you want to get to her, and you play your instrument just to get that person. That get you in trouble. I can look back at the old days when my daddy and them would play, and I didn't understand why all them fights and stuff would break out. 'Cause somebody play a guitar real well, and they get to playing to a certain guy's girlfriend, and there you go! 'Cause, now, if you a musician, a man—especially if you a front man—these men don't like you already. They think their women will like you. It's the same thing with a woman. If a woman is a singer, and she's real good. There's some women out there who already don't like her.

R.L. Boyce

Most kids today want that rap. I ain't with that rap stuff. All that "bumpty bumpty bump." I ain't with that s---. Blues always going to be different from rapping. Now, bell bottoms may come back, but the rappers going to be out the way. Like me and you, if I got a wife and you got one, and they done did us wrong, and you going down the road. You going to rap to her or you going to blues to her? [Laughs.] *You going to blues to her. You ain't going to rap to her. We don't need no rapping. The bell bottoms going to come back. The rapping's going to stay over yonder. You know what? When I come along, we come up the hard way. This rapping come up the short way. You know what I'm saying? You get home, the old lady done made you mad or something.* [Sings.] *"Babe, I'm so sorry. I'm so sorry. Won't you please try me one more time?" See? You ain't going to rap to 'em. Works every time. Right now, if my wife makes me mad, I get my little guitar and amp, and I go way in the other room. She tries to follow. "Go back, go back. For your own good. Let me do my little song here." And boy, I get that guitar and I'm fine. Get in the bed. Lay down and go on to sleep.*

BILL "HOWL-N-MADD" PERRY
(ABBEVILLE, MISSISSIPPI)

Here in Mississippi, my daddy was like a "Mississippi hustler," I guess you'd have to say. He sharecropped. He worked in the woods, cutting pulpwood, working the sawmills. But he also made moonshine, so that kind of supplemented his income. My mother did domestic work. That went on until '57, '58 or something like that, when my daddy stopped sharecropping and decided that he was going to just work in the woods and the sawmills. But then in 1961, my momma said, "I've had enough. I'm going to Chicago." So, like a bunch of other folks, we migrated to Chicago. I started learning chords and stuff like that before I left Mississippi, so let me back up a little bit. See, I told you that my daddy was a moonshiner, so that meant that we had plenty of company. There was this one guy, Ned Boles, that could really play. Now, Ned, if he was still alive, he would be in his nineties. He was right along with Robert Johnson and all those guys, and in fact, they all played together at one time or another. This guy would sit down there and start drinking that moonshine, and that sound, I mean, I've still got it in my head. I've never been able to duplicate like they did it. But I took what I felt and brought as much of it as close to my own original sound. The last time I saw Ned Boles was probably 1958 or '59.

R.L. BOYCE

I was born in 1955. You know what? I take care of myself. I do my little drinking. Go home and go to bed. Get up the next morning and work. Don't do no kind of drugs. When I was coming up, it was the cotton fields. Back then people were picking cotton and corn, sorghum molasses. Right down by my house. So hot, boy, I get out there, aw man, stripping them stalks. [Sings] "Lord, don't let the sun shine in the morning. If you just let it rain one more time, I'll be all right in the morning. Don't you dare let the sun shine one more time" [laughs]. Oh yeah, sing to make the time pass. [Sings.] "Lord if you can let me make it one more time 'til the sun goes down Friday, I'm going to juke with you in the morning, oh just let me lay down, so I can get that woman one more time." You don't know nothing about that. [Sings.] "I just ain't no good if I can't get that woman one more time." We played hard back then. Times was rough.

Red Paden stares out on Sunflower Avenue as he awaits his weekend crowd on a balmy night in Clarksdale. *Lou Bopp.*

MARTIN "BIG BOY" GRANT

You know it was the Hill Country—trance music. So, whenever you get on moonshine and Hill Country blues, you get a lot of people just swaying to the music and feeling it. The songs at Junior's could go on for thirty or forty minutes, you know. There was one old lady who would always sit there in the corner, and she would wait 'til Junior Kimbrough played "All Night Long," before she'd go home. It could be four in the morning, but she would want to stay to hear her song. If he played it first, she could leave early. If he played it last, she'd stay all night long. She was always there, every Sunday I was out there. It was such a fun time. I just miss it so much.

100 MEN DBA HALL

The 100 Men DBA Hall stands near the railroad track just a few blocks from the Gulf of Mexico in Bay St. Louis, Mississippi. From 2008 to 2017, it featured "live" blues and roots music with some regularity, following an impassioned, post–Hurricane Katrina renovation. Before that, way before that, it led a busy life—a life that is now in transition.

As I write these words, the ancient structure stands quiet and unassuming in the warm Gulf breeze. Only the Mississippi Blues Trail marker out front gives visitors a hint of the history that was made inside. With a little luck, the future may well be bright for the Hall, but more on that later.

The story of the Hall is at once familiar and yet quite unique. On the one hand, it's a classic American story of a people pulling together resources for the greater good of the community. On the other hand, it is a remarkable, distinctly African American story of an indigenous music giving hope and inspiration to future generations as it slowly spread to the rest of the world.

The story begins before the building itself but would have been lost to time if not for the enduring structure. Like the Apollo in New York or the Buena Vista Social Club in Havana, the 100 Men DBA Hall is both a source and a keeper of the flame.

The Home of the Blues

Unlike perhaps any other music short of gospel or classical, the history of blues and its family of subgenres and offspring (from jump blues to rhythm and blues and from jazz to soul) is often tied to particular buildings.

In the Mississippi Delta, it's the infamous juke joint—once a common sight on both cotton plantations and the "other side of the tracks" in town. In the bigger southern cities like New Orleans and Memphis, it's a Bourbon or Beale Street collection of ad hoc structures. Then there is the segregation-era brotherhood of venues affectionately labeled the "Chitlin' Circuit" that utilized geographically advantageous buildings to form a touring route for African American entertainers during those challenging times.

Regardless of size or ornateness, these buildings were places of socializing and entertainment during an era where whites and blacks couldn't always intermingle freely. In the case of the Hall, this was certainly true, although it was a whole lot more than *just* a good-time place for black southerners.

Even as rural blues styles have given way to urban modernism, musicians like "Duck" Holmes work to keep the old-school sound alive. *Lou Bopp.*

Ensuring (and Insuring) a Better Life

Blues music has been described as a "good man feeling bad" or "laughing to keep from crying." For the working poor who created the art form, it was a pressure valve that allowed folks to let off steam after a hard week and trade the drudgery of daily life for a night of music, dance and romance. Essentially, blues was, and still is, the poor man's psychiatrist.

To quote Buddy Guy's version of a Johnnie Taylor standard, "The people got money, still got a problem. Go to a psychiatrist to try and solve them. Any way you look at it—it's still called the blues."

Certainly, this is what the 100 Men DBA Hall transitioned into: a weekend dance hall and pressure valve, featuring all the great American-born music forms—blues, jazz, rhythm and blues, soul. But the Hall had a history even before that—even before the building that now acts as its history book.

Decades before the first nail hit the first board to build the Hall itself, its founding fathers formed the 100 Members' Debating Benevolent Association. According to the original 1894 bylaws, it was set up to "assist its members when sick, bury its dead in a respectable manner and knit friendship." Essentially, it was an insurance policy for the then uninsurable—impoverished African Americans.

Fortunately for music fans, the founding charter also expounded on the "knitting of friendship" by adding that the association could "from time to time give entertainments for the purpose of replenishing the treasury."

By the time the current structure was built in 1922 (first as an open-air venue and later an enclosed one), this association and its new building were set to administer to both the physical and mental well-being of the community.

Weathering the Storms through Time

Unlike many other societies throughout history, we Americans seem to tear down and replace many of our buildings every few generations whether we need to or not. This means that any history tied to those buildings is lost unless some historian at the time deems it important enough to canonize in writing. Of course, sometimes Mother Nature also lends a hand.

In the case of the Hall, we have an exception to the rule. Regardless of wear and tear, storms and strife, the old guard and new generation, somehow the archaic wooden structure survived decades of trends and teardowns (not to mention time spent as a bingo hall), only to meet a destructive force named Katrina in 2005. That fateful hurricane wiped many historic structures on the Mississippi Gulf Coast off the face of the earth, and it left the Hall in absolute shambles. Windows, doors, wiring, roofing—it needed everything fixed or replaced.

Abandoned by locals and seemingly less vital than the basic infrastructure that needed rebuilding in the wake of the storm, the Hall could have easily been cleared away from both the public eye and consciousness, if not for a few "outsiders" captivated by the past.

Founded by local black men generations ago, the Hall was purchased in 2006 by a transplanted white couple—California natives Jesse and Kerrie Loya. With more mission than money, they slowly restored the Hall to its original glory with the help of a generous grant from the Mississippi Department of Archives and History. The result of money, muscle and mission (and more than a few heated "discussions" between the couple) was reopened with much fanfare as a blues venue in 2008.

At the dedication of the (renamed) 100 Men Hall's Mississippi Blues Trail Marker in 2011, musician Deacon John captured the community's feelings this way: "I'm overwhelmed with joy from seeing the 100 Men Hall rise like a phoenix from the years of neglect and the ravages of storms to become the shining star of the Gulf Coast. This is not an ordinary building. This place has a unique history in the evolution of jazz, gospel, blues and rhythm & blues music—the only true American music. The music that transcends race, class, culture, gender, disabilities. The music that all of us love so dearly."

Why didn't the Loyas just let the city carry the Hall away to the landfill of history? Or, in an age of prefab pole barns and cookie-cutter constructions, why didn't they just replace it with something cheaper? The answer lies in the music and its history.

Blues, Jazz, R&B, Soul and Beyond

In many ways, the Hall could only have been born in Mississippi—a land steeped in blues. It also sits just sixty miles east of New Orleans—a party place known as much for classic rhythm and blues as the beginnings of jazz.

And both locales rejoiced in the early strains of African American gospel. So it should come as no surprise that the Hall of yesterday was a mix of these related genres—always with a basis in blues, the precursor to rock-and-roll.

The music of the Hall was made for dancing and socializing. It wasn't the lowdown, juke joint blues of the Mississippi Delta. Customers didn't sit at tables drinking moonshine and gambling as a lone bluesman played in the corner. By and large, these were bands that often included piano and horns in addition to guitars and drums. Back in the day, there were few tables to take up valuable dance floor space, and most of the chairs were lined up against the wall. When folks walked through the doors at the Hall, they were dressed up and ready to dance to the music 'til the wee hours of the morning.

Many of the Hall's acts are forgotten, but area fans and musicians recall a cavalcade of legends that included Fats Domino, Little Richard, B.B. King, Big Joe Turner, Guitar Slim, Etta James, Joe Tex, Earl King, Ernie K-Doe, Professor Longhair, James Booker, Irma Thomas, Eddie Bo, James Brown, The Nevilles, The Meters, Tyrone Davis, the Isley Brothers, Deacon Brown and many others. Local favorites also performed regularly, although it was the bigger acts—the ones with hit records—that drew the biggest crowds.

Blues and its offshoots all breathed life into the Hall and its enthusiastic clientele. Unsurprisingly, it even became a stop on the legendary Chitlin' Circuit.

Part of the So-Called Chitlin' Circuit

Whereas the Mississippi Delta and Hill Country regions were known for a culture of juke joints and house parties for "smaller" or more rural blues acts, another venue—a circuit of venues, really—developed to support "larger," more urban blues (and later R&B and soul) acts. It was affectionately known as the Chitlin' Circuit.

Named for perhaps the most soulful of soul food—chitterlings, aka cooked pig intestines—the Chitlin' Circuit was, according to Merriam-Webster, "a group of theaters and nightclubs that cater to African-American audiences and feature African-American entertainers."

According to the USDA website, "chitterlings (more commonly called "chitlins") became a traditional winter food of the American Deep South during Colonial times when, before refrigeration, hogs were slaughtered in

December. Those not living 'high on the hog' were given the less desirable parts of the animal."

In 2014, Preston Lauderbach, author of *The Chitlin' Circuit and the Road to Rock 'n' Roll*, told NPR, "The Chitlin' Circuit was African-Americans making something beautiful out of something ugly, whether it's making cuisine out of hog intestines or making world-class entertainment despite being excluded from all of the world-class venues, all of the fancy white clubs and all the first-rate white theaters."

The 100 Men Hall served as one of these "beautiful," distinctly black venues until the times slowly changed.

THE HALL, THE CIRCUIT AND TODAY

So what does the future hold for the Hall and the circuit? While there are no guarantees, as I was working on this book, a forward-thinking African American writer from New Orleans purchased the Hall with plans to once again breathe new life into the old structure.

According to south Mississippi's *Sun Herald*, "New owner Rachel Dangermond said she plans to operate 100 Men Hall as a multi-purpose venue and add writer workshops, retreats and artist in residency programs. Dangermond said she also sees it as a place for pop-ups, community dialogues, youth activities, rehearsal space and as a filming location for the movie industry." Stay tuned. Fortunately, the final history 100 Men Hall can't be written quite yet.

As for the Chitlin' Circuit itself, it is much less active—much less needed—these days, in part because of modern access to what would have been "white" venues back in the day and in part because of evolutions in music and media.

In the larger cities, particularly in the South, the African American blues tradition has largely evolved into a less downhome, more urban sound. Deejays and record labels call the healthiest of the culturally connected music "southern soul." Generally speaking, it is a soulful, contemporary R&B sound often backed by modern studio electronics and fronted by adult-themed lyrics.

In bigger cities, these acts that would have historically played the Chitlin' Circuit in the past now play the same arenas, auditoriums and casinos that rock, pop and country acts do. Only in some of the smaller towns do the old venues roll on.

A Music Moves On and On

In 2003, I attended a "Christmas Blues Show" at the Clarksdale Civic Auditorium. It was a revue featuring several "live" bands and short sets, playing everything from traditional blues to the soul blues of the day. The impeccably dressed crowd was 99 percent African American and mostly middle-aged on up.

In 2015, I once again attended a "Christmas Blues Show" at the same auditorium. Wow, what a difference. The audience was still 99 percent African American, but it was a bit younger and dressed much more casually. There were six acts, but only three of the acts had "live" bands. The other three were simply men who came out and sang their southern soul radio hits over backing tracks played on the PA. The music was almost entirely contemporary. There was no "traditional" blues. One of the "live" bands did play some classic soul blues (e.g., Tyrone Davis and Johnnie Taylor). They were my personal favorite but actually garnered the least amount of audience applause.

Blues music and its exponents often brings people together from sometimes disparate worlds. *Lou Bopp.*

I relate this anecdote not to judge what is or isn't blues, and definitely not to judge the age or dress of the audience, but only to illustrate how the music, audience and staging of culturally connected, African American "blues" has evolved in modern times. After all, art and audiences must evolve to stay relevant in a culture.

That said, I'll leave you with the thoughts of an older African American radio deejay who moved to Clarksdale from Los Angeles in the early 2000s, the late Steve Ladd: "Some guy wrote that once we left the projects and went to the boulevard, we forgot from which we came. As far as the music goes, that's true in so many instances. It's like that with the African-American community everywhere. Bobby 'Blue' Bland and Ike Turner, they had orchestration with horns. Now you've got these musicians doing soul blues, and they've got a machine playing horn lines. We take our listeners for granted that they don't know. But they know. They can hear it. It's like a cheap shot of music, I think."

And so the music and venues (and opinions) evolve as time marches on.

TAKING JUKE JOINTS ON TOUR

While writing the book you now hold in your hands, I took a week off to bring a bluesman to Israel for a few shows. I'd met the promoter, Yamit Hagar, half a dozen years earlier during Clarksdale's Juke Joint Festival, and since then, she'd worked hard to bring Mississippi's best juke joint players to the Promised Land.

These weren't necessarily the names Israeli music fans already knew. They were the names they needed to know—juke joint names, including Robert "Wolfman" Belfour, L.C. Ulmer, Terry "Harmonica" Bean, James "Super Chikan" Johnson and Robert "Bilbo" Walker, among others.

Through radio interviews, TV appearances, newspaper features, film screenings, workshops, guitar giveaways, concerts and festivals, Hagar—along with a handful of partners in Israeli music and media—has slowly helped to build a base of fans, knowledge and opportunity for juke blues in the Holy Land.

BORN TO PLAY THE BLUES

This time around, Hagar asked me to bring Clarksdale's true-blue torchbearer—thirty-four-year-old Anthony "Big A" Sherrod. Big A is an amazing musician and performer. He is also the strongest living link to the past three decades of Clarksdale's deep blues culture of weekend juke joints and house parties.

He started playing at five and a half years old and went on to play bass, drums and guitar with all of the major blues figures here. His early gigs were as an underage kid in dark, smoky, very adult spaces and places. Like a sponge, Big A soaked up all that he heard from his mentors. He learned what did and didn't "work" with the hard-drinking, boisterous and often unforgiving juke joint audiences. And he got good. Really good.

Today, he is like a human jukebox and known for his dynamic, high-energy shows. Like a history lesson, his lengthy sets often include songs he learned firsthand from Clarksdale-area stalwarts such as "Mr. Johnnie" Billington, "Dr. Mike" James, "Little Jeno" Tucker, "Miss Gladys," Wesley "Junebug" Jefferson, Terry "Big T" Williams, "Big Jack" Johnson, Robert "Bilbo" Walker and James "Super Chikan" Johnson. A tourist once told me, "It's like the music is just flowing through him," and others have also marveled at the "feeling" in his music.

While he has loads of technique and an impeccable sense of tuning and timing, he is not about reproducing songs note for note. In fact, he is the opposite. He often deconstructs classics, improvises new rhythms and melodies or creates brand-new songs on the spot. In the world of juke joints, as Red's Lounge owner Paden says, "You've got to get in where you fit in." In other words, you have to roll with the (sometimes literal) punches and, again as Red says, "go beyond the call of duty."

Through the years, I've seen Big A both back and lead bands at jukes in Clarksdale and vicinity such as Smitty's Red Top, Rivermount Lounge, Blues Station, Po Monkey's Lounge, Do Drop Inn, Margaret's Blue Diamond, Annie Bell's, Delta Blues Room, Big T's Blues Spot, Sarah's Kitchen, Club 2000 and Red's Lounge. His mentors didn't use set lists (since many of them lacked the education required to write one, frankly), so he grew up playing one song at a time and then reading the audience reaction and deciding what tune to plunge into next. That's "juke joint style."

On the Israeli tour, Big A played three shows three nights in a row. Because of cancelled and rescheduled flights, we arrived in Tel Aviv a day late and missed the scheduled rehearsal with his new Israeli rhythm section. That made me nervous, but he seemed unperturbed.

He met his bassist and drummer for the first time on stage at the soundcheck for the inaugural Sderot Blues Festival that he was headlining. Hager cleared the soundcheck schedule so the trio could turn it into a bit of a rehearsal. Big A did two quick songs for soundcheck, and seeing that

Since quitting his factory job to concentrate on playing blues, Terry "Harmonica" Bean has traveled to Europe and beyond. *Lou Bopp.*

the soundman was good with the levels and his backing musicians were top notch, he walked off the stage. No rehearsal necessary. No set list allowed.

In the three nights of shows that followed at the festival, a cultural center and a club, Big A only repeated one song in nearly six hours of music—just one song. He debuted new originals and played the classic covers he'd learned from his Clarksdale mentors. At most, he signaled the key to his musicians before launching into the next mystery tune. And it sounded amazing. The sellout crowds demanded encores in each and every setting.

Another juke joint technique he employed was taking the music and the show to the audience. He walked out into the crowds, playing long, improvised guitar solos thanks to his wireless guitar setup, as he posed for selfies and danced with the ladies. He also talked to audience members personally from the stage, just like back home in the juke joints.

Juke Joint Adventures from the Road

Working in the sometimes underground, always entertaining world of Mississippi blues since 2002 has afforded me many almost unbelievable experiences. As always, I am not just talking about a musical genre called "blues" here. I'm talking about a living, breathing culture—a juke joint culture. It is not just the Mississippi blues musician and his or her bag of songs that goes on tour; it is everything that man or woman has experienced in life and music, including the attitude necessary for survival in the largely poor Mississippi Delta. With these instant house party characters, you pack everything but the juke's kitchen sink into each and every trip.

Some of the travel tales here come from halfway around the world. Others are a bit closer to home. Hopefully, all shed a little light on why blues is still relevant both in and out of the Saturday night juke.

New York City Gets the Blues

Flying into New York's LaGuardia International Airport with bluesmen James "T-Model" Ford, Terry "Harmonica" Bean and Lee Williams, I chuckled to myself. As the flight attendant came over the PA to announce our landing, I was reminded of Leland, Mississippi bluesman/folk artist Pat Thomas talking about the only time he ever stepped foot on an airplane. He'd been invited to represent his late blues-playing/folk artist father, James "Son" Thomas, at an exclusive art gallery showing of his dad's work. All he knew was that he was flying to "New York," so when the lady on the PA announced, "Welcome to LaGuardia," the younger Thomas jumped up from his seat, shouting, "Welcome to Maguala?! Maguala?! I'm supposed to be going to New York!"

For this trip with T-Model (then in his late eighties) and crew, a Brooklyn-based music/dance nonprofit had my buddy Jeff Konkel and me set up a Mississippi Blues Week, featuring the three characters I had in tow plus Jimmy "Duck" Holmes and Robert "Wolfman" Belfour. Konkel would fly with Duck, and the Wolfman would fly with himself to the Big Apple.

While the shows were all in Brooklyn, the organizers had a hotel sponsor in Manhattan, so we stayed at a pretty slick, pretty high-end high-rise. As we waited in line at the check-in counter, T-Model suddenly started trying to get the attention of a man two people ahead of us in line by poking him with his cane. As I tried to quietly stop him, T-Model loudly announced, "Hey, I know you. I know you. You run the corner store in Greenville!"

Embarrassingly, T-Model was convinced that the only other gentleman he'd apparently ever seen of Middle Eastern heritage was the same man who runs the little grocery in his own native Greenville, Mississippi. He was excited to see his friend from back home. The culture clashes had begun.

The next morning after breakfast, some of us in our group wanted to go out and explore Manhattan. Not the old bluesman. When we arrived at his room, T-Model said he just wanted to go downstairs and sit in the lobby. We took him down in the elevator and suggested a nice, quiet corner by a window. Oh no, he wanted to sit in the luxurious leather seating that faced the big, automatic sliding doors at the main entrance of the swanky New York hotel.

When we returned from our explorations (and a quick sushi lunch) a few hours later, there was T-Model still sitting there in his fresh little dress-casual outfit and beanie-type hat. He seemed to have enjoyed himself. The hotel staff later told us why. The whole time we were gone, T-Model had propositioned every woman who walked in after the *swoosh* of the sliding glass doors. His technique?

"Hey...*hey!*"

"Yes, may I help you?"

"Are you married?"

According to the smiling staff, this basic exchange was repeated over and over with no apparent success.

Late that afternoon, we had to gather the band together and catch a ride to Brooklyn for a show at Frank's Cocktail Lounge. Since we had three musicians and their gear plus Konkel and me, we opted for a van. I was afraid to break the group up into two cabs since "a quick stop for a drink" might have resulted in some lost bluesmen.

Now, I'm not sure if cutting through Chinatown is *the* way to go to Brooklyn or not, but it is *a* way. As we crawled through Chinatown in rush-hour traffic, the younger musicians had their flip phones out to snap pictures of the Chinese-language neon signs and exotic-looking pedestrian traffic. T-Model, who was sitting in the front seat next to the driver, took it all in for a minute before slowly turned around with an odd look on his face.

"Oh no," I thought, as I braced myself for something potentially disparaging and archaic to come out of the octogenarian's mouth.

In what felt like slow motion, T-Model declared, "Would you look at allllllll...............the Mexicans!" The van erupted in laughter. No, this wasn't a slur. He wasn't trying to offend anyone. It was simply a lack of proper vocabulary. To T-Model, anyone didn't look like us, anyone who wasn't a "Mississippian," was obviously "Mexican." (To be fair, geography never really was his thing. He once told me he was "going overseas" to play a festival. I asked where. "Canada," he replied.)

That night, Frank's cool little jazz spot in Brooklyn turned into a hot little juke joint—almost literally. So many folks jammed into the place that we were all sweating, and at one point, I felt lightheaded and had to stand up from my seat jammed in a corner just so I could catch my breath. It was amazing. Red's, Po Monkey's and the rest had been successfully transported to the big city, if for one night only.

BIG GEORGE HITS BIG TIME...AND THE ROAD

Soon after I relocated from St. Louis to Clarksdale, I started booking shows for bluesman "Big" George Brock. He had migrated from a cotton plantation near Clarksdale to North St. Louis back in the late 1950s but loved to return home to his native Magnolia State for shows whenever possible, so I would bring him down when I could.

Booking shows led to recording albums, which led to making a documentary, which led to taking the big man overseas—first to Italy and Switzerland and later France and the United Kingdom.

When Big George met me at the Memphis International Airport for our two-week trip to the United Kingdom, he brought enough suits, hats and shoes to outfit most of the royal family. We spent twenty sweaty minutes in the parking lot editing down his wardrobe selection. The challenge was that each suit had its own matching hat, shoes and, in some cases, vest or belt.

Big George was also insistent on bringing his own personal DVD player/ screen combo and a small library of vintage cowboy movies. Of course, the electrical current is different overseas, so his player wouldn't work. Amazingly, our tour host actually had the same portable player made to work in Europe. So, the bluesman's favorite old-time cowboy royalty, Rocky Lane, rode again.

On the first night of the two-week UK tour, Big George (or in his version of the story, yours truly) forgot his stack of color-coordinated hats (one for each suit) at the hotel. It took a week for a few lovely female fans to catch up with the big man in New Castle to reunite the hats with their suits, so for a week, Big George was forced to wear his "travel hat"—a somewhat ratty old straw fedora—regardless of the brightly colored suit.

Going through post-9/11 airport security was always an adventure with Big George, of course, since he wore enough bling to stock a pawn shop—multiple gold rings, bracelets, a necklace, a watch, fancy glasses and more. He also had a special walking cane that lit up when you put downward pressure on it. The problem was that the light was broken and didn't light up, so you can bet that the security agents had fun taking that instrument of bluesman terror apart for inspection at each stop.

Perhaps the most surreal night I spent overseas with Big George was on a trip to France. After the gig, we sat together in his small hotel room, just outside Toulouse, watching the best of the worst we could find on TV. It was a horrible *Predator* movie sequel made all the less satisfying by the fact that it was overdubbed in French. Still, we sat there glued to the tiny TV screen trying to decipher what was being said. Eventually, I went out and walked around 'til I found a bar that would sell me some beers to go. The movie definitely improved upon my return.

WE JUKE UP IN HERE! CARAVAN CRASHES GENEVA

Here's the scenario. One bluesman had never flown overseas. Another didn't like European food. And the third? Well, sometimes I think he'd rather drink than eat.

Armed with this knowledge, my blues buddy Konkel and I crossed our fingers, said a prayer and proceeded to book a Mississippi-to-Switzerland blues caravan one fateful August. The plan was to screen our *We Juke Up in Here!: Mississippi's Juke Joint Culture at the Crossroads* documentary and present some of the players featured in it.

We had a fine conspiratorial team in the Rootsway Roots & Blues Association of Parma, Italy. The organization helped us get the hookup with the Geneva Arts Festival. And what a hookup it was.

Each August, the festival assembles a huge temporary amphitheater for one month of major concert and film events. It had an enormous stage, complete with a drive-in size screen behind it. The seating was stadium style, and the backstage green rooms consisted of a series of attached trailers. Built for rock stars, we filled the venue with three of the most downhome Delta bluesmen we know: Terry "Harmonica" Bean, Jimmy "Duck" Holmes and Louis "Gearshifter" Youngblood.

The night before our film screening and concert debut, reggae-rap star Shaggy packed the house. When our two nights were done, Kool & the Gang took to the stage. (The Gang checked out our second night, incidentally, although they seemed more bewildered by it than anything as they ate their dinner off Styrofoam plates high up in the cheap seats.) But I'm getting ahead of myself. Let's back up.

While the plane tickets may have been purchased, when you are dealing with juke blues characters from Mississippi, I'm here to tell you that there are absolutely no guarantees of anyone with a guitar or harmonica getting on the airplane. Phone numbers, addresses and agreements are always subject to last-minute change.

To begin with, Duck had only ever flown once before (to New York City, on a really rough flight) and had turned down many previous offers to fly across the big pond. And then there's the fact that of the seven of us going (Jeff, me, three musicians and our two movie cameramen, Damien Blaylock and Lou Bopp), none of us even live in the same town.

You may think you know "iffy"? Well, we know iffy. Somewhat surprisingly—though not without many phone calls and a seriously sleepless night—everyone made it to the Memphis airport. Everyone even remembered passports.

The flight over was actually pretty good. Harmonica Bean hit on the stewardesses, Duck slept like a champ and Gearshifter drank. However, upon our arrival, we learned that some of our luggage had gone left when we went right.

An experienced world traveler, our buddy Bopp was just short of tracking down the president of the airline in search of his missing camera bag while Gearshifter took on a generally depressed demeanor as he stared at the empty baggage carrousel going 'round and 'round. *All* of his luggage was missing.

The next morning, I came downstairs at the hotel in search of coffee and breakfast. I was greeted by a slightly scruffier Gearshifter—still in his travel outfit—eating a bowl of potato chips and drinking a beer. He was pondering the fate of his luggage.

This pondering lasted for another bowl of potato chips and two more beers as the rest of us woke up to caffeine and muesli. Later, he had the "worst beer" he'd ever tasted from his room's mini-bar. Upon closer examination, we informed him that it was actually a very expensive—if mini—bottle of brut champagne. His trip was starting out a little rocky.

On our first night of shows, we arrived early at the concert/film venue and took all the guitars back to the green room trailers. They were outfitted comfortably with chairs, tables and—wait for it—adult beverages. Yes, the first night, mixed in with the bottled waters and soda cans, there was a surprisingly tasty selection of beers in all of the trailers.

To be fair, our musician friend Gearshifter was nervous. Back in Mississippi, he rarely plays outside his hometown, and he'd only been overseas one other time, a decade earlier. Fortunately, he's a professional. He's a man who can handle his booze.

You may have noticed that I said there were beers (plural) backstage on the first night. Well, let's just say that after *someone* finished all of them off, they restocked very lightly for the second night. Still, and this is the honest truth, Gearshifter played amazingly both nights. The first night he attacked the blues, diving in headfirst from the get-go. The second night was a slow smoldering burn but every bit as effective.

Aside from his aversion to the event's non–soul food dinner, Harmonica Bean was absolutely turn-key as usual. We wound him up and pointed him toward the stage, and he took over. Once again, he proved an energizing performer and people person. Duck, on the other hand, won over his audience with his mesmerizing, deep, gutbucket blues groove. He brought his Blue Front Café juke joint vibe from Bentonia, Mississippi, to the shores of Lake Geneva. We concluded each night with the trio of Gearshifter, Duck and Harmonica jamming out a song or two together.

Initially, there was some trepidation—and a lot of trash talk—about this encore jam since only Duck and Harmonica had played together previously, and Gearshifter's style might be considered relatively more modern. But the excitement (or was it tension?) that resulted really pushed it over the top, making both encores unforgettable highpoints.

Once the encore applause died down, we screened our juke joint film featuring these fine bluesmen and others, and those in attendance juked up in there.

Geneva, Switzerland's *We Juke Up in Here!* concert and screening featured some well-stocked "green rooms" for artists. *Lou Bopp.*

Jimmy "Duck" Holmes grooves while bigger-than-life *We Juke Up in Here!* images by Lou Bopp project in the background. *Lou Bopp.*

Talking "Geeses" on the Way to Philly

In 2013, artist/musician Stan Street and I took septuagenarian blues rocker Robert "Bilbo" Walker along with Robert "Wolfman" Belfour and Anthony "Big A" Sherrod to perform on WXPN's *World Cafe Live* radio show in Philadelphia, Pennsylvania.

On the drive from Clarksdale to the Memphis airport, we saw hundreds of migrating geese in some of the sprawling cotton fields running alongside Highway 61 North. It got Bilbo thinking. During our layover in Atlanta, he told us a hilarious story that could only come from the mouth of a juke joint bluesman. Pardon the dialect, which he really played up; I'm simply trying to do his storytelling justice:

> *I was driving on Delta Avenue one day, just out from downtown Clarksdale. I looked out to my right, and said to myself, "I'll be darned. Look at all those geeses. There must've been a hundred of 'em." I said to myself, "I'm gonna get me some!"* [He made a motion with his hands as though twisting a neck.] *So, I drove my truck into this park where they were and noticed they weren't afraid of me, so I drove right up to 'em. I got out, real slow-like, and they just let me walk right out into the whole pack. So, I'm looking for some big ones and thinking about how I'm going to* [acts out twisting their necks] *like this, you see. I got way out into them. Boy, there was a whole bunch of geeses. Suddenly, one of the geese—he must've been the leader—signals the others. He yells, "Aww! Aww!" and they all started attacking me! They came from everywhere, jumping on me, biting me and trying to pull me down into the pack. I was fighting them off, and I'll tell you the truth, now. Lord, I thought if they pulled me down, they were going to kill me! I fought my way back to my truck with them hanging on me, tearing up my paints, bloodying up my suit.* [He acts out trying to run in water.] *I finally got back in my truck, and they'd hurt me now. Pulled meat off me! I drove straight down to the police station and reported them. And do you know what those policemen did? They laughed at me!* [Bilbo laughs.] *They laughed. And then the game warden came down and told me I shouldn't have been messing with them to begin with—something about "poaching" being illegal. Uh huh. So now, today, whenever I see some geeses, if I've got my gun, I just shoot at them to get revenge for the ones that attacked me. They all know each other, you know.*

That night at the hotel in Philly, the whole band dined together. It was a Chinese restaurant, so after watching Stan and me for a few minutes, Bilbo sat down his fork and attempted to use chopsticks. That elicited almost as much laughter as his story about the day he got goosed, although the restaurant staff was perhaps slightly less amused by the cleanup.

Heavy Blues Meets Heavy Beef in Brazil

Speaking of Bilbo, I took him to Brazil once for a two-week tour, starting in Recife and ending up in Porto Alegre. We ate out every night, and like clockwork, Bilbo would always eat about half of his meal and request a doggie bag for the rest. He'd take it back to his hotel room, get up in the middle of the night, heat it up in the microwave and enjoy a second feast.

The final night of the tour, he ordered what was essentially a chicken-fried steak. As was his habit, he bagged up half of his meal and took it back to his room. The next morning, as we sat in the hotel lobby awaiting transport to the airport for our flight back to America, he turned to me and said, "You know, the strangest thing happened to me last night." "Oh yeah?" I replied, "What happened?"

> *Well, I woke up about two in the morning and thought about those leftovers. Mmm hmm, that was some good dinner. So, I pulled that steak out of the fridge, put it in the microwave and hit some buttons. But nothing happened. I hit some more buttons, and nothing happened. Then, I couldn't get the door of the microwave back open. I still couldn't when I got up this morning. I sure did want that steak!*

I'm like, "Huh?" because I knew our rooms didn't have microwaves. I asked a couple more questions and then burst out laughing—as did Bilbo. Turns out he'd locked his leftovers in his hotel room safe and pushed some of the numbers on the front hoping to turn it on. We laughed about that all the way back to Clarksdale and on every trip we took after that. I can't even imagine what the maid must have thought when she opened that safe only to find heavy beef.

The Wolfman Meets the Actor

In 2005, I booked North Mississippi Hill Country blues legend Robert "Wolfman" Belfour on the Rootsway Blues & Food Festival in Italy—an excellent event.

On the morning of our return flight home, the driver showed up late at our rural B&B, so when we hit the airport, we were in a state of panic, rushing to try and make the plane.

In the hurry to get the Wolfman a wheelchair and obtain our boarding passes, airline officials tried to separate us. (The secret I'd learned from traveling with ancient bluesmen? Always stick with the old man in the wheelchair. Airports always take care of him.) A young Italian lady was "assigned" to us and got us running through the airport. She was brand-new to her job and, honestly, didn't know what she *couldn't* do.

As we disappeared into the bowels of the airport, we evaded public security and even waltzed through a clandestine room full of startled pilots smoking and playing poker. Finally, we hit our only security zone—one apparently maintained for pilots and legends. I say this because when I looked up from my sweaty, out-of-breath haze, there he was. Ernest Borgnine, the actor. He seemed as startled by our sudden appearance as we were by his, but he was jovial and smiled just like in the moving pictures. (Borgnine had a lot in common with some of the older bluesmen I've known, by the way. He was married five times and made it to ninety-five years old, entertaining fans for more than six decades.)

After that bewildering, slow-motion respite, we ran off again. Finally we were standing at a wall of towering glass windows looking out on a sea of parked planes. The young lady picked up what seemed to be a random phone on the wall, got into an Italian yelling match with someone, hung up, smiled nervously at us and waited. Suddenly, through the sea of planes came a transport vehicle straight out of sci-fi—an elevator on wheels. It pulled up to a glass door that I hadn't previously noticed and raised the "elevator." An unhappy-looking dude opened the door. We stepped in, and after some very quick and debatable instructions, he stepped off, leaving our young lady at the controls. (There was also a driver in the cab below us whom she could communicate with by phone, thankfully.)

There we were—sweating, convinced we'd missed our flight and preparing to perish as our young lady tried to figure out the buttons of our wheeled elevator. Our crazy vehicle took off, weaving through a mess of trailers, trucks and planes. Finally, we came up to a big jetliner—on the side opposite of where you normally enter as a regular passenger. After a bit of experimentation and some additional yelling into a phone, the young lady raised us up like an elevator to the emergency exit behind the cockpit. As God is my witness, the door suddenly popped open!

We stepped onto the plane like we owned the place. Well, ok, perhaps the look on the crew faces didn't exactly give us that feeling. But we'd made it just the same. And we'd met Ernest Borgnine. Two nights later, the Wolfman was back at his favorite Clarksdale juke joint, still chuckling about our airport adventure.

Speaking of airplanes, on another trip—this time to Norway on an *M for Mississippi* caravan—the Wolfman was joined by fellow bluesmen James "T-Model" Ford and L.C. Ulmer. Our flight from Amsterdam to Notodden was the worst flight I have ever personally been on, with the plane doing dead drops for what felt like an eternity and passengers screaming. After ultimately landing upright, my buddy Konkel leaned over to T-Model and joked, "Well, that was a little bumpy." Without missing a beat, T-Model replied loudly, "Bumpy? Bumpy? That weren't bumpy. Ridin' a mule—*that's* bumpy!"

THE LANGUAGE OF FOOD LOST IN TRANSLATION

I arranged for Terry "Harmonica" Bean to play in Italy for a week and stay at the same rural B&B that the Wolfman and I had stayed at the week before. Upon his return, I asked Bean if he'd enjoyed all of the amazing Italian food. His answer cracked me up:

> *Well, I'll tell you. When I go back, I got to carry me some Viennas* [i.e., cheap canned sausages]. *I got to have room in my suitcase for that. I mean, man, I can't eat that food over there. It just don't fit me. I'm a soul food eater. I was raised up on neckbones and pigs' feet and cornbread. Stuff like that. I ain't the kind of guy that'll try anything. I can eat one thing all year 'round, just keep eating the same thing. I can. I don't want to try nothing. You can't get tired of something that is good to you. I got to have those Viennas, man.*
>
> *Now, the* [prosciutto] *ham over there, it was all right, but* [the hostess at the Italian B&B] *kept bringing it real thin. It was thinner*

than tissue, and you had to fold it up just so you could feel it, man. You pull it out like that, it ain't nothing. But you fold it up, then you got a little something. I was trying to tell her, "More ham," but she didn't know what I was talking about, and I didn't know what she was talking about. I was trying to tell her I wanted a big piece of ham, and she didn't know what I was talking about because she speak Italian. Well, she went back to the kitchen, and I went with her. The ham was right there, and I pointed at it, and she was saying, I guess, "That's ham." But I was talking about, "I want a piece of ham." Well, when she done that, I thought she was saying it was OK, so I took the knife, and I cut me a big hunk off—a big ole piece of ham. Well, she didn't like that, 'cause I could look at the expression on her face. She didn't like that. I know, 'cause they had a lock on the door after that! [Laughs.]

Proof that you can take the bluesman out of the juke joint, but you can't take the juke joint out of him.

SEARCHING FOR A LOST BLUES WEEKEND

A North Mississippi bluesman by the name of Odell Harris showed up at my Cat Head store in Clarksdale, Mississippi, one day. I had a little blues fest going that afternoon, and he showed up looking for a mutual friend, Steve "Lightnin'" Malcolm.

Odell's fascinating blues style and crazy rapport with his audience immediately pulled me in. He also sat in that night at Red's juke joint, showing off even more of his magnetic personality and enigmatic style—just like he apparently used to do at Junior Kimbrough's old juke when it was still a thing.

The next day, I told my buddy Konkel at Broke & Hungry Records how great he was, and Malcolm later confirmed it. Fortunately, as his record label name may infer, Konkel is just crazy enough to set up with a recording session with a guy he's never heard or met in a place he's never visited. And so, a weekend recording session was planned in south Mississippi.

To ensure that he'd be in good shape for such an undertaking, Konkel (who lives in St. Louis) started with a late-night blues and booze show in Memphis that Friday night, catching what was left of juke joint favorites,

The Fieldstones. He arrived in Clarksdale on Saturday looking a little rough but ready for a road trip.

Five hours later, we arrived in Ocean Springs, Mississippi, at a little blues and BBQ joint. Odell was booked to play an early evening show there with Malcolm, so the plan was to make a "studio-quality field recording" in the inside bar area after the audience left.

Everyone seemed surprised when Odell Harris actually showed up for the gig. He was a bit of blues character after all—one who enjoyed his own chaos and didn't always want to be found (think witness protection program).

Around 10:00 p.m., the outdoor public show ended. By about 11:30 p.m., the tapes were rolling inside the bar turned temporary recording studio. The positive vibes and anticipation were palpable. Initially. By 1:00 a.m., tempers were flaring, expletives were flying and fists were on the verge of being thrown.

In my own defense, the venue owner and his friends' girlfriends *were* making a lot of noise—too much noise for a recording session. And then one of them dropped her keys. Loudly.

Mississippi's Jimmy "Duck" Holmes, Terry "Harmonica" Bean and Louis "Gearshifter" Youngblood prepare to blues Geneva. *Lou Bopp.*

Konkel maintains to this day that you can hear me *shush* the young ladies on the final album. Regardless, things got real tough real fast with threats of kicking my derriere, trashing our equipment and more. Ultimately, after I agreed to no longer speak a word inside the building, we were left alone to finish the recording session.

The deep blues rumbled on gloriously as night turned to day. Finally, around 7:00 a.m., the tape ran out, literally. The grueling all-night recording session was complete, even though none of us knew for sure if there was really an actual "album" in the can. (Let's just say that Odell liked to sing in the opposite direction of the mic, switch up tunes mid-song and laugh, a lot.)

When Konkel went to pay him. Odell stared at the check like he'd never seen anything but cash in his whole life. Then, he honestly said, "Oh, you don't have to pay me." (Something you will never, I repeat never, hear another juke joint player say in your life.) Of course, he took the check, and it cleared the bank by Monday afternoon.

We'd booked hotel rooms in town but elected not to use them since the night had completely slipped away. Instead, we all agreed to pack up, pull ourselves together and meet at an area Denny's in half an hour for a celebratory breakfast.

That was the first and last time Konkel ever saw Odell Harris. Apparently, Ocean Springs has more than one Denny's. Who knew?

Turns out that there *was* an album in the can—one heck of an album. Broke & Hungry Records released it in under the appropriate title, *Searching for Odell Harris*. Sadly, Harris passed away a few years later, living off the grid in extreme southern Louisiana.

Relationship Therapy, Delta Blues Style

One of my favorite things about living Mississippi is that I can hang out with my blues musician friends with some regularity.

A year or two after my relocation to Clarksdale, I called the Greenville home of blues legend James "T-Model" Ford, thinking I might take the day off and drive down for a visit. His girlfriend, Miss Stella, answered. We small-talked for a minute before I asked, "How's T-Model?"

Miss Stella got dramatically quiet and responded, "Oh, you didn't hear?" (Pause, for effect.) "We're not together anymore." I said all the things you say after such a statement, trying to cheer her up. Finally, after a couple minutes of contributing factors from her and sympathies from me, I started my exit from the conversation, saying something like, "Well, hang in there, and I'll talk to y'all later."

But as I rushed to hang up, Miss Stella asked, "Well, don't you want to talk to T-Model?"

"Huh?"

"He's right here," she said, matter-of-factly. Sure enough, T-Model was sitting across the room the whole time while Miss Stella was on the phone, pushing his buttons. (To be fair, T-Model probably had it coming. He *was* a bit of a rabble rouser himself.)

A few hours later, I walked through the front door of T-Model's house. As he and I sat two feet apart in the living room making conversation, Miss Stella sat across the room, whispering a laundry list of T-Model complaints to her girlfriend on the other end of the beige, corded phone.

Finally, as if to say he'd had enough, T-Model turned toward me and said, "Gimme that thaang!" as he motioned to his faithful Peavey Razer electric guitar, affectionately named "Black Nanny." Warm, distorted chords slowly drowned out the phone call as T-Model grinned. Soon, he began singing, as he looked his lady straight in the eyes from across the room: "I should'a quit you babe, long time ago…." T-Model Ford, aka the "Great Communicator." I guess that's the difference between folks who sing the blues and folks who *are* the blues.

The occasional feud aside, T-Model and Miss Stella were together for many years and did eventually get married. She took care of him on his sickbed 'til the end, and some of my favorite blues memories in life involve visits to their various homes—the first of which was in an old, single-wide mobile home. They always made me feel welcome—even that day.

A T-Model and a Grappa Walk into a Bar…

On my first trip to Italy with "Big" George Brock, we traveled with our old chum James "T-Model" Ford, who was represented by Fat Possum Records at the time.

After the last show of the Italian tour, ole T-Model introduced himself to something called grappa. Basically, it was a bottle of 120-proof moonshine made from grape skins, stems and seeds. While his young road manager was, let's just say, busy with some lovely local ladies, T-Model spent the evening partying with his fans—and his grappa.

The next day at the hotel, we didn't see him for breakfast or lunch or dinner. His overindulgence kept him in his hotel room for an entire day and night. Fortunately, we just happened to have a whole day off before our flight back to the States.

When our shuttle van finally got us all to the airport more than a day later, T-Model, shall we say, left his mark on the parking lot. But in typical T-Model Ford fashion, by the time he was on the international flight home, he was bright eyed and bushy tailed, instinctively hitting on all of the attractive stewardesses. After all, the six-time-married father of twenty-six kids was almost as proud of his self-proclaimed "ladies' man" moniker as he was his ability to hold his alcohol (domestically, at least).

Never one to be shy, T-Model was known to look at a happy couple from the bandstand and say to the woman, "I'm just sorry I know your husband." His mischievous grin, laughing eyes and advanced age let him get away with a lot. He would also look at the man and say, "If you love your woman, you better put a stamp on her, because if you don't, and she flags my train [pause for effect], I'm gonna let her ride!"

Getting Caught in a Blues Fishing Trip

Late one night in 2002, I got into a fishing discussion with the proprietor of a juke joint called Blues Station. The owner, local guitar hero Terry "Big T" Williams, started bragging about how the catfish he was catching were "this big" (picture two hands held generously apart).

His "this big" was a helluva lot bigger than my "this big," so I said, "I want to go fishing with *you*!"

"I'll pick you up at your house tomorrow morning at 8:00 a.m.," he promised. At 9:00 a.m., I was still waiting on my front porch, fishing pole in hand. Finally, I heard a tell-tale rumble and backfire as his old pickup came into view. He pulled into my driveway with few words exchanged, and off we went.

"You had coffee yet?" he asked. "Yes, thanks." I wanted to add, "Two hours ago" but refrained. He pulled in beneath the golden arches. Apparently, he hadn't had *his* coffee—or Egg McSandwich yet. I paid, of course, since he drove.

Next, he announced, "We need bait." Soon, we were in a grocery store parking lot. I'm thinking, "Since when are there worms in the freezer section?"

Oh no. Apparently, to catch the big ones, you have to drop fifteen dollars on frozen shrimp. ("Couldn't we just eat the shrimp and call it a day?" I asked.) I paid, of course, since he drove. And drive he did, way out into the Delta countryside. Then he turned left, and suddenly we were there.

We pulled into what turned out to be—and I'm not making this up—a Mennonite-owned catfish farm *pay lake*! (No wonder the fish were "this big.") Half an hour later, we had more than enough enormous catfish. The nice lady at the gate weighed them and handed us the bill. I paid, of course, since Big T drove.

We headed home. Well, not exactly. On the drive back, Big T cut through a tough neighborhood (as in "the 'hood"), announcing that we'd need to find "a crackhead who needs cash" to clean our catch cheaply. (For those who don't know, catfish do not have scales; they have a tough-to-remove skin in addition to sharp spikes in their fins.) Conveniently, we found a random, kind of scary guy wandering the streets who claimed to be an expert catfish skinner.

We all rode to Big T's juke joint, Blues Station, where T informed me that I needed to go get a "catfish skinner." I'm thinking, "Isn't that the guy we just picked up?" But no. Apparently, there was an actual tool of the same name. The scary guy was simply the man who would use the tool. So, off to Wally World I went. I paid for it, of course, since T did most of the driving. Oh, I paid for the other—human—catfish skinner too. Obviously.

Big T told me (and my empty wallet) to go home, relax and come back in two hours to pick up my share of the catfish haul, so I did. Two hours and ten minutes later, I was fitting a big, bulging bag of fresh fish into my refrigerator.

I was super excited about making dinner that night. I pulled the catfish out of the fridge, made up a bowl of seasoned cornmeal, heated up my cast-iron skillet and smiled. This was going to be great. Then I opened the Ziploc.

Oh, it was full of catfish all right—in much the same way fish sticks are full of fish. Lots of fins and tails. I cursed. I laughed. I fried. It was darn tasty, though—even at thirty dollars a pound. Sometimes you don't have to hop a flight to have a juke joint adventure that's out of this world.

JUKE JOINT FESTIVAL

On January 28, 2004, Clarksdale businessman Bubba O'Keefe came bursting through my front door at Cat Head. As the door slammed behind him, he walked quickly and with purpose toward my counter and spoke:

> *"That idea we've been talking about?"*
> *"Yeah?"*
> *"Let's do it!"*
> *"I'm with you, Bubba. Now, which idea?"*

A STAR FESTIVAL IS BORN

When I first started visiting Clarksdale in the mid-1990s, there wasn't much to see, do or hear for a blues-minded tourist. There was one very small blues museum and maybe one or two blues shows on average per week—though no real way to know about them 'til you arrived. Some Saturday nights were wholly silent.

There was one blues festival here at that time—excellent but in the sweaty, buggy month of August. And there was one very cool little blues record store with casual hours that later closed for good.

The town and surrounding countryside were steeped in blues history, obviously, but at that time, there were no plaques or monuments to document Clarksdale's rich musical past.

Formerly the "Golden Buckle on the Cotton Belt," Clarksdale's downtown business district—the heart of the city—was once so bustling that there were one-way streets to control traffic flow, multiple traffic lights and restrictive two-hour parking signs. By the late 1990s, the heartbeat had slowed. The two-hour parking signs still stood but were no longer enforced. You could park wherever you liked. By the time I moved here in 2002, the patient was on life support. If I left my store an hour late at the end of a weekday, I could often look both directions down Delta Avenue and not see even one parked car.

It was during my visits prior to moving here that O'Keefe and I started to talk about what was and what could be. We started to talk about the potential of blues and cultural tourism. The heart was still here. The beginnings were in place, but they needed a serious jolt.

Juke Joint Festival is the year's biggest business night for Red's and other little jukes and clubs in Clarksdale. *Lou Bopp.*

A "Mad Man" with the Blues

I was based in St. Louis at the time, living an ad man's life—working crazy hours, making crazy money and taking business trips around the world. But even while living the proverbial American Dream, I kept driving south for every vacation, every long weekend—to my Clarksdale dream.

During those repeated, year-round visits, I would always run into O'Keefe somewhere—sometimes at a lunch place, other times on a street corner. Always we talked, dreamed and schemed.

Of course, early on in my quest for blues history and music, I was as likely to visit Greenville, Leland or the North Mississippi Hill Country as I was Clarksdale. I made friends and acquaintances throughout the region so that whenever I returned, even if there was no festival action during the day or juke joint music at night, I had something to do, someone to visit or some blues to hear. If old bluesmen like T-Model Ford or Willie Foster didn't have gigs out, then I would just visit them at home.

Through the years, I slowly found myself more and more in Clarksdale. The other towns I visited just didn't seem to have the same vibe and infrastructure as Clarksdale, and they damn sure didn't have a cheerleader like Bubba O'Keefe.

O'Keefe and I often discussed why music fans from around the world trickled through this decaying Delta town. What was the appeal? What were they doing here, and how long were they staying?

These visits and discussions led me to the "mission" that ultimately caused me to drop out of corporate America—a mission to "help organize and promote the blues from within." A mission mostly based around the concept that if we were the town with the "live" blues at night, then we would be the town to get the overnight visitor who was traveling through what we now call the Americana Music Triangle—an ad hoc collection of music stops between Nashville, Memphis and New Orleans.

When I first moved to Clarksdale, bringing my advertising/marketing/branding background and extreme blues fandom with me, most of the tourists I met in my blues store were what I coined the "two-hour visitor to Clarksdale." These folks may have known about the Delta Blues Museum or might have heard that legends like Muddy Waters and Ike Turner grew up here, but honestly, they could see everything blues-related in about two hours back then. For most nights of the week, even on a good week, there was little, if any, pre-scheduled "live" blues that you could plan on.

The blues shows that did happen were typically on the weekend and very spur of the moment, largely word of mouth—not very helpful to a tourist on the road, especially in that era before social media. (No Facebook or Twitter. No Google or Yelp. No smartphones or tablets.)

You could luck into an occasional Thursday night show at Sarah's Kitchen or a Saturday night jam at Red's Lounge, but they might just as well be quiet when you rolled into town. It was a roll of the dice back then.

Even after Morgan Freeman's Ground Zero Blues Club opened—which enthusiastically emulates the look and feel of a classic juke joint—its music was just Friday and Saturday and not always blues. That said, the club was absolutely a big step forward for our little town. Freeman's name brought many a fan (and more than a little media) through the doors. Seeing the club's potential for growing tourism, I handled the blues bookings from 2003 to 2010, expanding its reliable, marketable music nights to four, including occasional shows by juke joint favorites like David "Honeyboy" Edwards, Willie King, James "T-Model" Ford and "Big Jack" Johnson.

"That Idea We've Been Talking About?"

This brings me back around to O'Keefe marching into my store in 2004. We'd talked about the many things Clarksdale needed to become a tourist town, to truly become "Bluestown, USA." We needed more nightly music. We needed more annual events. We needed better hotel accommodations. We needed espresso-based coffee. We needed beer offerings besides Bud and Bud Lite. We needed (and still need) better ground transportation.

As a bold first step toward these many goals, we envisioned a spring festival to kick off the season, celebrate blues history, promote local venues and showcase the potential of our rustic downtown.

I had started hosting two small Cat Head Mini Blues Fest events per year and assisting with the blues bookings for our town's only other music fest at the time—a wonderfully downhome event called the Sunflower River Blues & Gospel Festival, which is still held each August. So, I'd dipped my toe in the festival water.

O'Keefe burst through my door that fateful day to tell me that our concept for Juke Joint Festival—"half blues festival, half small-town fair

At the end of the day, Clarksdale's Juke Joint Festival aims to put more business into businesses—like Red's Lounge. *Lou Bopp.*

Blues fans arrive for the theatrical premiere of the *We Juke Up in Here!* doc during Juke Joint Festival in Clarksdale, Mississippi. *Lou Bopp.*

and all about the Delta"—was a go. He had convinced our local First National Bank to loan us the starter money for a year, which was all we needed to move forward.

The concept was simple. Create and maintain a festival brand that would:

- appeal to both insiders and outsiders, locals and tourists
- highlight our region's rich juke joint history
- feature our living, breathing Mississippi blues music
- showcase our then nearly empty, bee-trapped-in-amber downtown
- show visitors southern hospitality; show locals the world loves us

Simply holding "another blues festival" wouldn't be enough. After recruiting a handful of like-minded locals who saw the vision (including Nan Hughes, who is today one of the event's main organizers), our nonprofit put "live" blues on some small stages downtown in the daytime and in a few juke joint venues at night. We also rented bus shuttles to move fans around at night and minimize drinking and driving. We did this for safety and also to help the venues make more money by selling more beer.

If marketed properly, the blues events would bring the tourists. But what about the non-blues fan locals? What would make these folks visit their mostly empty downtown and sit next to international tourists for what was ostensibly a "blues" festival? Two words: racing pigs.

Additionally, our new "blues festival" featured a petting zoo, arts and crafts, southern food and more. Eventually, we added an entire kids' zone, as well as perhaps our biggest non-blues attraction, the Ghost Riders—monkeys riding dogs herding sheep from Pontotoc, Mississippi. (Yes, you read that correctly.)

Of course, plenty of locals wanted to experience the music, too, but we needed Clarksdale's "old money" and young families to attend the festival as well the regular music fans. We needed to boost the town's morale, visually explain the benefits of tourism and reintroduce potential investors to our wonderful infrastructure of classic downtown buildings. That part of the festival planning we referred to as our "secret mission"—the mission to mix excited tourists with friendly locals. And it worked.

It worked so well that after a few festivals, former tourists from around the United States and the world started moving here—musicians, artists, entrepreneurs, retirees and others. Then a handful of locals started buying empty buildings downtown—opening restaurants, renovating retail spaces and constructing overnight apartments. Juke Joint Festival was not the only factor in these decisions, but it is the one most mentioned to this day by tourist transplants and downtown business owners.

Nearly a decade and a half into the event, volunteers polled attendees to find out how wide the festival's reach had become. They documented visitors from at least twenty-eight foreign countries, forty-six U.S. states and fifty-three Mississippi counties. The event has helped to put our town on the map and the "juke joint" into a broader, global context. It has also become a benchmark for how some other regional festivals organize their events.

At Its Heart, It's Still About the Jukes

Of course, this is a book about juke joint culture, of which the festival is now part.

The first year of Juke Joint Festival, I dropped by Red's Lounge on Saturday night to pay the bandleader—the late, great Wesley "Junebug" Jefferson—and while I was waiting for him to get off mic, one of our festival shuttle buses pulled up out front. It dropped off a group of five, very senior citizen white ladies. These were ladies who grew up in a time of segregation, a time when they would have never even considered waltzing into a traditionally black juke joint.

That night, however, they were "protected" by a festival wristband and delivered by an official shuttle bus. In other words, the juke's doors were wide open, and they were there to party.

This may seem like a one-off thing, but regardless of whether or not these members of the Golden Girls generation ever went back to Red's during a non-festival period or not, they had crossed a cultural threshold and lived to tell about it. Now, hopefully, they *would* tell about it. Word of mouth is a powerful thing. It can motivate footsteps, and it can win hearts and minds. It's words like those that have given legs to the festival and helped to make our local jukes a bit more respected.

In advance of the festival that first year, O'Keefe and I split up and gave talks at all of the local civic group meetings—Kiwanis Club, Exchange Club, Rotary Club, Lion's Club and more. At one of the clubs that I addressed, a member stopped my talk when I mentioned Red's Lounge.

At first, he didn't believe that it was still open, still a viable business. (Admittedly, to this day, even when it's open, it pretty much looks closed.) When I assured him that it was, even if it wasn't featuring as much music as it once did, he then went on to challenge the safety of the venue.

Now, when I say this, I mean it. But I don't mean to offend anyone by saying it. Since my time as a tourist in, and later a transplant to, Clarksdale, I have only ever seen bar fights in so-called white venues. Nothing major—frankly, mostly just frat kids getting into it—but still.

What makes an authentic juke joint a safe place in modern times is that the owner takes no fuss. He takes care of business because he knows his quasi-legal establishment could easily be shut down if problems occur, especially since today's crowds are a mix of locals and tourists. So, to see that crew of lovely older ladies come off the bus that first year and into the juke really meant something. It meant progress.

No, Juke Joint Festival hasn't "saved the juke joint" (or the blues inside) from extinction. Jukes still close; old bluesmen still die. But the festival has provided a foundation to work from to bring back a downtown and to provide blues musicians and juke and club owners

Bentonia, Mississippi's Jimmy "Duck" Holmes is regular act at Clarksdale's annual Juke Joint Festival. *Lou Bopp.*

with positive business opportunities. It has helped to hip many locals to our town's potential and announced to the world that culture still matters—blues music still matters.

As Australian economist John C. Henshall said in his recent study of our town's blues (and juke joint) comeback, *Downtown Revitalisation and Delta Blues in Clarksdale, Mississippi: Lessons for Small Cities and Towns*, "This is a story about Clarksdale and the economic revitalisation process that led to the rebirth of the city's downtown after many years of decline and dereliction…[through] blues music…cultural tourism."

In Conclusion (For This Volume, Anyway)

If you close this book and open the door at a place like Red's Lounge tonight, you will step back in time. You will walk out with not only a smile on your face but also a better understanding of what "blues" really is—both the music *and* the culture. But don't wait.

There are very few long-running, authentic, "live" blues juke joints left. Come find them while you still can. Plan your Delta blues pilgrimage today with help from the following sites:

www.jukejointfestival.com
www.msbluestrail.org
www.americanamusictriangle.com
www.visitclarksdale.com
www.visitmississippi.com

Also, please check out my Music Calendar and Clarksdale Guide webpages on my Cat Head store site (www.cathead.biz). Then, to paraphrase Palmer again in *Deep Blues*, "Come see how much history can be transmitted by pressure on a guitar string."

BIBLIOGRAPHY

BOOKS

Bond, Dr. Beverly G., and Dr. Janann Sherman. *Images of America: Beale Street.* Mount Pleasant, SC: Arcadia Publishing, 2006. ISBN 9780738543635.
Brewster, Bill, and Frank Broughton. *Last Night a DJ Saved My Life: The History of the Disc Jockey.* New York: Grove Press, 2014. ISBN 9780802146106.
Calt, Stephen. *I'd Rather Be the Devil: Skip James and the Blues.* Chicago: Chicago Review Press, 2008. ISBN 9781556527463.
Cheseborough, Steve. *Blues Traveling: The Holy Sites of Delta Blues.* Jackson: University of Mississippi Press, 2008. ISBN 9781604731248.
Cobb, James C. *The Most Southern Place on Earth: The Mississippi Delta and the Roots of Regional Identity.* New York: Oxford University Press, 1992. ISBN 0195089138.
Dalzell, Tom, and Terry Victor. *The New Partridge Dictionary of Slang and Unconventional English.* United Kingdom: Routledge, 2014. ISBN 9780415212588.
Davis, Francis. *The History of the Blues: The Roots, the Music, the People.* New York: Da Capo Press, 1995. ISBN 0306812967.
Graves, Tom. *Crossroads: The Life and Afterlife of Blues Legend Robert Johnson.* Memphis, TN: Devault-Graves Agency, 2012. ISBN 9780988232204.
Guralnick, Peter. *Lost Highway: Journeys and Arrivals of American Musicians.* Columbus, GA: Little, Brown and Company, 2013. ISBN 9780316332743.

Henshall, John C. *Downtown Revitalisation and Delta Blues in Clarksdale, Mississippi: Lessons for Small Cities and Towns.* Australia: Palgrave MacMillan, 2018. ISBN 9789811321078.

Kay, Jackie. *Bessie Smith.* Bath, Somerset, UK: Absolute Press, 1997. ISBN 1899791701.

Lauderbach, Preston. *The Chitlin' Circuit: And the Road to Rock 'n' Roll.* New York: W.W. Norton & Company Inc., 2011. ISBN 9780393076523.

Lomax, Alan. *Land Where Blues Began.* New York: New Press, 2002. ISBN 1565847393.

Martin, Scott C. *SAGE Encyclopedia of Alcohol: Social, Cultural, and Historical Perspectives.* Thousand Oaks, CA: SAGE Publishing, 2015.

Merriam-Webster English Dictionary. Revised 2004. ISBN 087779930X.

Oakley, Giles. *The Devil's Music: The History of the Blues.* New York: Da Capo Press, 1997. ISBN 0306807432.

Oliver, Paul. *Blues Off the Record: Thirty Years of Blues Commentary.* New York: Da Capo Press, 1984. ISBN 0306803216.

———. *Conversation with the Blues.* United Kingdom: Cambridge University Press, 1997. ISBN 9780521591812.

Palmer, Robert. *Deep Blues: A Musical and Cultural History of the Mississippi Delta.* New York: Penguin Books, 1981. ISBN 0140062238.

Segrave, Kerry. *Jukeboxes: An American Social History.* Jefferson, NC: McFarland & Company Inc., 2002. ISBN 9780786411818.

Stolle, Roger. *Hidden History of Mississippi Blues.* Charleston, SC: The History Press, 2011. ISBN 9781609492199.

Weems, Robert E., Jr. *Desegregating the Dollar: African American Consumerism in the Twentieth Century.* New York: New York University Press, 1998. ISBN 9780814793275.

Magazines/Journals/Newspapers

Brown, Luther, Dr. "Inside Poor Monkey's." Southern Spaces (June 22, 2006). www.southernspaces.org.

Gorman, Juliet. "What Is a Jook Joint?"/"Cultural Migrancy, Jooks, and Photographs." *New Deal Narratives* (May 2001). www.oberlin.edu.

Hammond, John, Sr. "Did Bessie Smith Bleed to Death While Waiting for Medical Aid?" *DownBeat* (1937). www.downbeat.com.

Bibliography

New York Times. "Paul B. Johnson Jr. Dies at 69." October 15, 1985. www.nytimes.com.
Nillson, Jeff. "1969: The Post Listens to 'The Soul Sound.'" *Saturday Evening Post*, August 5, 2010. www.saturdayeveningpost.com.
O'Neal, Jim. "Clarksdale Moan: The Evolution of the Blues in Coahoma County." *Living Blues.* www.livingblues.com.
Perez, Mary. "Historic 100 Men Hall Has New Owners and They Want to Shake Things Up in the Bay." *Sun Herald* (August 5, 2018). www.sunherald.com.
Shoofly Magazine/Bay St. Louis Living. "Men Hall: A Community Treasure" (September 2012). www.bslshoofly.com.
Skelton, B.J. Bessie Smith article. *Press Register*, October 3, 1957. Courtesy of WROX Museum, Clarksdale, MS. www.pressregister.com.
Stolle, Roger. "Big George Brock." *Blues & Rhythm Magazine* (2006). www.bluesandrhythm.co.uk.
———. "Cat Head Blues Mississippi." *Twoj Blues* (various issues). www.twojblues.com.
———. "Cat Head's Delta." *King Biscuit Time* (various issues). www.kingbiscuittime.com.
———. "Delta Journeys." *Blues Music Magazine* (various issues). www.bluesmusicmagazine.com.
———. "Down in the Delta." *Blues Revue* (various issues). www.bluesrevue.com.
———. "Greetings from the Historic Riverside Hotel." *Blues Festival Guide* (2008). www.bluesfestivalguide.com.
Stolle, Roger, ed. *Delta Magazine* (various issues). www.deltamagazine.com.
Time. "Mississippi: Bourbon Borealis" (February 11, 1966). www.time.com.
Woodruff, Nan Elizabeth. "Mississippi Delta Planters and Debates Over Mechanization, Labor, and Civil Rights in the 1940s." *Journal of Southern History* (May 1994). www.jstor.org.

Song References

Jones, Booker T., and William Bell. "Born Under a Bad Sign." *Born Under a Bad Sign.* New York: Warner/Chappell Music Inc., Universal Music Publishing Group.

Taylor, Johnnie. "Still Called the Blues." *Johnnie Taylor on Malaco, Vol. 1*. Composed by Earl Forest, George Jackson, R.A. Miller and Robert Miller. Arranged by Buddy Guy. Jackson, MS: Malaco Records, 1976. www.malaco.com.

HISTORICAL MARKERS

Mississippi Blues Trail markers (Blue Front Café, "Rocket 88," Hopson Commissary, 100 Men Blues Hall, Po Monkey's Lounge and Riverside Hotel). Mississippi Blues Commission, 2009. www.msbluestrail.org.

OTHER REFERENCES

American Experience. "Sharecropping in Mississippi: The Mississippi Delta." PBS, TV broadcast/website, 1996–2018. www.pbs.org.

Brock, Big George. *Hard Times* DVD documentary. Cat Head Presents, 2006. www.cathead.biz.

Brown, Tanya Ballard. "The Origin (and Hot Stank) of the 'Chitlin' Circuit.'" *Code Switch* radio program, NPR, 2014. www.npr.org.

Davies, Lawrence. "New World Jukebox Blues." *All Thirteen Keys* blog. King's College, London, July 24, 2015. www.allthirteenkeys.com.

Great Big Story. "If You Build It, They Will Come: A Juke Joint's Field of Dreams." New York: Turner Broadcasting System, 2017. www.greatbigstory.com.

M for Mississippi. DVD documentary. Three Forks Music, 2008. www.mformississippi.com.

The Mississippi River of Song. PBS, Filmmakers Collaborative and the Smithsonian Institution, 1998. www.pbs.org.

Moonshine & Mojo Hands. Documentary series. Three Forks Music, 2008. www.moonshineandmojohands.com.

Murphy, Josh, and Roger Stolle. *Juke Joint Kings*. Unreleased reality show video pitch tape, 2014.

Pine, Joseph, and Guy Raz. "Is Authenticity Real?" *TED Talk Radio Hour*, NPR, 2014. www.npr.org.

Smith, Dr. Hugh, letter to B.J. Skelton. *Press Register*. Remembrance of Bessie Smith accident, August 27, 1957. Courtesy of WROX Museum, Clarksdale, MS.

USDA. "Food Safety Education: Yersiniosis and Chitterlings." www.fsis.usda.gov.

We Juke Up in Here! DVD documentary. Three Forks Music, 2012. www.wejukeupinhere.com.

INDEX

A

Abel, Bill 45, 111
Apple, Sean "Bad" 51

B

Bean, Terry "Harmonica" 44, 59, 76, 122, 134, 137, 141, 147
Belfour, Robert "Wolfman" 53, 114, 134, 137, 144, 146
Blaylock, Damien 77, 141
Blue Front Café 25, 26
Bopp, Lou 9, 77, 141
Boyce, R.L. 48, 51, 113, 117, 122, 124
Brenston, Jackie 88
Brock, "Big" George 47, 76, 88, 109, 139
Broke & Hungry Records 7, 150
Brown, Luther 75

C

Carr, Sam 43, 47
Cat Head Delta Blues & Folk Art 7, 17, 40, 62, 77, 81, 86, 94, 100, 148, 154, 157
Cheseborough, Steve 23, 28
Chitlin' Circuit 127, 130, 131
Clarksdale, Mississippi 7, 17, 84, 94, 155
Climmie's Western Inn 10
Cummings, "Blind Mississippi" Morris 112

D

Davis, Cedell 44, 110
Deep Blues Festival 27
Delta Center for Culture & Learning (Delta State University) 75
Durham, David Lee 107

Index

E

Edwards, David "Honeyboy" 64, 109, 113

F

Ford, James "T-Model" 43, 115

G

Gip's Place 25, 26
Grant, Martin "Big Boy" 49, 50, 52, 106, 125
Green's Lounge 7
Grimes, Larry 78

H

Hagar, Yamit 134
Hammond, John, Sr. 81, 83
Harris, Odell 148, 149, 150
Henshall, John C. 162
Hidden History of Mississippi Blues 9, 22
Hill, Z.L. 86
Holmes, Jimmy "Duck" 25, 26, 59, 108, 118, 121, 141
Horton, John 43, 45, 58, 105
Hughes, Nan 159
Hurston, Zora Neale 24

I

Ingram, Christone "Kingfish" 120

J

Jackson, Mary Ann "Action" 51, 52, 58, 113, 116
Jefferson, Wesley "Junebug" 55
Johnson, "Big" Jack 57
Johnson, James "Super Chikan" 106
jukeboxes 28, 29
Juke Joint Festival 7, 27, 157, 160, 161

K

Kimbrough, Robert, Sr. 48, 64, 121
Konkel, Jeff 8, 65, 77, 137

L

Ladd, Steve 55, 133
Lauderbach, Preston 131
Lomax, Alan 82

M

Malcolm, Steve "Lightnin" 49, 117, 118
Malvezzi, Guy 119
Massey, Mark "Mule Man" 112
M for Mississippi 8
moonshine 62, 63, 64, 65, 66, 68, 70
Moonshine & Mojo Hands 8, 65
moonshiner 62, 65, 66, 123
Moore, Sarah 56

INDEX

N

Negro Motorist Green Book, The 87
Nighthawk, Robert 89
Nolden, "Cadillac" John 42, 97, 116

O

O'Keefe, Bubba 84, 154, 156
Oliver, Paul 24
100 Men DBA Hall 126, 128, 129, 131

P

Paden, Red 18, 25, 41, 53, 54, 56, 94, 119
Perry, Bill "Howl-N-Madd" 123
Pine, Joseph 10
Po Monkey's Lounge 71, 73, 75, 76, 77, 78
Potts, "Dr. Feelgood" 110

R

Ratliff, Frank "Rat" 86, 87, 93
Red's Lounge 25, 26, 94, 120, 157
Riverside Hotel 85, 86, 87, 89, 92
"Rocket 88" 88, 89
Rootsway Roots & Blues Association 140

S

Seaberry, Willie 71, 75
segregation 23, 81, 85, 87, 91, 127, 160
sharecropping 21, 22, 23, 33, 53, 66, 71, 123
Sherrod, Anthony "Big A" 120, 134
Smith, Bessie 81, 82, 83, 84, 85, 87, 88
Spires, Bud 109, 115
Stewart, Josh "Razorblade" 57
Sunflower River Blues Festival 27

T

Teddy's Juke Joint 25, 26
Turner, Ike 88

U

Ulmer, L.C. 107

W

Walker, Robert "Bilbo" 31, 134, 135, 144
We Juke Up in Here! 8, 77, 96, 140
Wild Bill's 25
Williamson, Sonny Boy, II 88, 90
Wonder Light City 30, 32, 34, 35, 36, 38, 39, 40

Y

Youngblood, Louis "Gearshifter" 54, 61, 114, 141

ABOUT THE AUTHOR AND THE PHOTOGRAPHER

ROGER STOLLE has owned Cat Head Delta Blues & Folk Art—Mississippi's blues store in Clarksdale—since 2002. His first book for The History Press was *Hidden History of Mississippi Blues*. He is a *Blues Music Magazine* and *Twoj Blues Magazine* columnist, *Delta Magazine* contributing editor, former blues radio personality (Sirius-XM Bluesville, WROX, KDHX), Coahoma County Tourism Commission member and festival cofounder (Juke Joint Festival, Clarksdale Caravan Music Fest, Clarksdale Film Festival and more). Stolle has produced several critically acclaimed blues CDs/DVDs (such as *Big George Brock*) and coproduced the documentaries *Hard Times*, *M for Mississippi*, *We Juke Up in Here!* and *Moonshine & Mojo Hands*. Stolle's Cat Head store has been called "one of the 17 coolest record stores in America" (*Paste*), is included in the book *1,000 Places to See Before You Die* (Workman Publishing) and received a Keeping the Blues Alive Award (Blues Foundation). He was educated at the University of Cincinnati and worked for thirteen years in the advertising and marketing world before entering the world of blues music and juke joint culture. www.cathead.biz.

LOU BOPP is a commercial photographer by trade. He came to blues as a music fan and has photographed a majority of the significant living Mississippi blues musicians in recent years. Bopp was educated at the University of Missouri and traveled the world on assignment for clients such as Time Warner, Deutsche Bank, McCann-Erickson, AMD, *TIME*, FutureBrand, Y&R and many more. His photographic work has taken him from the floor of the NYSE to the top of the Empire State Building, from the renowned sands of Iwo Jima to the legendary "Crossroads" of Clarksdale, Mississippi. In the blues music realm, Bopp has photographed everyone from James "T-Model" Ford to "Big" George Brock; he has gone from juke joint to house party and from pool hall to living room in search of his subject matter. His blues work graces the pages of *Hidden History of Mississippi Blues*, as well as an official U.S. postage stamp marking Mississippi's bicentennial and featuring Jimmy "Duck" Holmes. The human experience intrigues and fascinates Bopp, and his goal is to capture images that reflect the authenticity and meaning of this experience. Bopp currently splits his time between New York City, St. Louis and (at times) the Mississippi Delta. www.loubopp.com.

Visit us at
www.historypress.com

www.ingramcontent.com/pod-product-compliance
Lightning Source LLC
Chambersburg PA
CBHW042139160426
43201CB00021B/2343